# The Passion that Shapes Nations

## Charlie Cleverly

# Victor®

Kingsway Communications Ltd, Eastbourne, England
Cook Communications Ministries,
Colorado Springs, Colorado • Paris, Ontario

ISBN 1 84291 213 5

Victor is an imprint of
KINGSWAY COMMUNICATIONS LTD
Lottbridge Drove, Eastbourne BN23 6NT, England.
Email: books@kingsway.co.uk

Printed in the USA

# THE PASSION THAT SHAPES NATIONS

'The history of the persecuted church is remarkable and stunning as again and again She comes out victorious, albeit through blood, tears, pain and prayer. Charlie's book is both a reminder and a vital wake-up call for the church around the world to join hands and hearts and see our final victory realized.'

*John Arnott*
*Senior Pastor, Toronto Airport Christian Fellowship*

'Charlie Cleverly writes with fervour, compassion and conviction. He faces up the faithful believer with the high calling of martyrdom throughout history and presents a serious challenge for pending martyrdom confronting the western church today.'

*David Pytches*
*Author and speaker*

'Charlie makes a huge, unruly subject manageable and very accessible . . . presented in a deeply convicting way. We would like to make it compulsory reading for all new Christians.'

*Stuart and Celia McAlpine*
*Christ Our Shepherd Church, Washington DC*

'The church in the West is in great danger of conforming to the prevailing culture's self-centred goals of personal fulfilment and immediate gratification. This book comes as a reminder of genuine Christlikeness. In highlighting martyrs across centuries of Christian history it is a call to live like Jesus, to love like Jesus, and if necessary to die like Jesus – that others would have the joy of knowing God's love as we do.'

*John Coles*
*Director, New Wine*

This book is dedicated to
Reuben Samuel Bradley
and your future friends

# Contents

# Foreword

I wish to testify about Revd Charlie, a servant of God. He is a typical evangelical pastor, filled with confidence in God and love for people. He is down to earth. A loyal and honest person.

While he was preaching, I observed there was true love and mercy within him. He was indeed preaching the truth with boldness and love.

His preaching has brought comfort and encouragement to those who were hurt and weary, so that they could rise up to follow Christ again.

He impressed me with a gentle and humble spirit. Particularly in some meetings, where I was invited as the speaker. I understood that he is a man with clean hands and right heart. He is a man who is trustworthy.

He and his wife have got great burden to get the overseas students saved. They are willing to obey the great commission even when there is a great price to pay.

Rev. Charlie is a gift that God has given to this generation. I believe his book will become an example for today's and future generations.

*His Servant, Bro. Yun*

# 1

## The Martyrs' Memorial

*'Jesus promised his disciples three things: that they would be
completely fearless, absurdly happy, and in constant trouble.'*
G.K. Chesterton

*'O friends, what about these heroic spirits? What about those
faces that look at you today through that blinding smoke and
those devouring flames? Look again at those martyr-men.
They stood up there before heaven and earth and spoke in the
loudest language that can be spoken for the truth and love
and cause of Jesus Christ.'* William Booth

*'We say we are Christians, we proclaim it to the whole world,
even under the hands of the executioner, and in the midst of
all the torments you inflict on us. Torn and mangled we cry
out as loud as we are able to cry: We are worshippers of God
through Christ Jesus.'* Tertullian

At the heart of England lies the town of Oxford. At
the heart of Oxford stands the Martyrs' Memorial.
Like the mast of a buried ship, it lies constrained,
fettered, quiet. It is unremarkable amidst the noise of the
traffic. Yet its message is prophetic and wooing. Every time
I look on it, as I do whenever I take visitors around the city,

I close my eyes and try to imagine the martyrs. This monument commemorates just three, but what a three. One was an archbishop: Thomas Cranmer. Cranmer was author of *The Book of Common Prayer*, eventually published in 1662, a majestic piece of literature which had almost as much influence on the development of the English language as the works of Shakespeare.

Let us pause and see if we cannot marvel or shed a tear at the thought of an archbishop and architect of the Reformation, primate of all England, head of the Privy Council, being led in freezing winds and black rags after long imprisonment to the public spectacle of death by burning.

A few weeks earlier he had been preceded by Bishop Latimer. As this unforgettable preacher went to his death, Hugh Latimer whispered to his companion the now famous phrase, 'Be of good cheer, Master Ridley, and play the man. We shall this day light such a candle, by God's grace, in England as, I trust, shall never be put out.' With this book, I am trying to keep that candle burning. It is a candle calling out for courage. It is a beacon to lighten our darkness. It is a fire burning to warm the hearts of young people to their destiny to be witnesses to the love of Christ in our land. It is, I hope, a trumpet to awaken those who sleep to their responsibility.

The word 'martyr', of course, has two meanings in the Greek from which it comes: there is first the idea of witness, and only second the idea of death. The fact was that among the first Christians, to be a witness led inexorably to arrest and then to death. Hence the elision of the two meanings in the one word, and now the idea of martyrdom has lost its link with witness.

In 2003 I moved with my family from Paris to Oxford to the pastorate of St Aldate's, a large community and student church at the heart of this historic city. Although the build-up to this call had been proceeding for years, I had no idea of the impact that such a move would have on Anita and me in terms of joining in with the travailing of the Holy Spirit.

The effect on us of being in a city where men were martyred for their faith in Christ only 500 years earlier, as well as communicating constantly with so many students who, we feel, have a destiny on their lives which may include martyrdom, is enough to make us pause and weigh our words. This book is dedicated to those dear students, whom we love.

Paris, of course, has also seen martyrs. At around the same time as the Oxford martyrs, under the influence of Catherine de Medici the St Bartholomew's Day massacre unfurled its fury in 1572, as no fewer than 10,000 people were killed in a wave of anti-Protestant persecution. The waters of the River Seine ran red with their blood.

In fact, every era of history has known those who have been witnesses and, as a result, martyrs. This book, sensing the prophetic time in which we live, is written with a desire to awaken courage and a sense of destiny, and to edify in remembering how these men and women lived. It is also written to bring to remembrance what they said. We shall take note of their lifestyle, and of the content and substance of their message, in order to be instructed in a day of much confusion. We shall find their message to be timeless and timely.

It is my conviction that this 'gift of courageous suffering' is being and needs to be restored today. We see it on the tear-stained faces of the forcefully advancing Chinese church. We see it in the nearly invisible army of love advancing through and suffering in Islamic strongholds of the 10/40 window. And yet where is the zeal, the passion, the downwardly mobile, radical, inevitable witnessing of the Church in the West? Sometimes it is there; but often we slumber, clogged with the clutter of materialism. The Church's concerns are so often to do with the comfort of the children in the crèche, the volume of the music, the length or style of the sermons. My prayer is: 'Deliver us from evil!' May God re-create, as so often before, but this time from all the Church if such a thing is possible, a lean Gideon's army to defy the world systems which gradually are clouding and thickening the very air we breathe, and gagging and shackling the Church into an intimidated silence. This silence is akin to that forced upon Esther. Her uncle Mordecai managed, with visionary words, to awaken her: 'Do not think that because you are in the king's house you alone . . . will escape. For if you remain silent at this time . . . you and your father's family will perish. And who knows but that you have come to royal position for such a time as this?' (Esther 4:14) My prayer is that this book may awaken us to courage and risk-taking as in the days of Esther.

Mark Stibbe writes, 'When the Holy Spirit descended on Jesus at his baptism like a dove, Jesus was enabled and empowered not only to perform signs and preach with authority. He was also anointed to give his life . . . He was endowed with the power for martyrdom as well as miracles.'[1]

Pope Paul II, when he preached in Paris in the year 2000 to nearly a million people, famously cried out in his faltering

voice, *'France, fille aînée de l'Église: qu'as-tu fait de ton baptême?'*
('France, older daughter of the Church, what have you
done with your baptism?') This book is a call to recovery of
our baptism inheritance: the capacity, nay even the desire,
to suffer for Christ.

It has been said that the Church is in every age in danger
of losing her apostolic DNA: that is to say, in danger of losing part of the character of what it means truly to be Christian. We can think of the holiness and evangelism restored
in the best moments of monasticism, the justification and
access to intimacy with Christ of the Reformation, the Revivals of the eighteenth and nineteenth centuries, the recovery of apostolic missions and the outworking of the Great
Commission from the nineteenth century, the outpouring
of Pentecostalism in the twentieth century, returning the
Church to her inheritance of 'receiving power and being
witnesses' and resulting in massive Pentecostal expansion
and influence on the worldwide Church.

At the dawn of the twenty-first century, what do we see?
God willing I would say we see a new baptism in sacrificial
love flowing from the Church. The prophetic ministry of
Mother Teresa caught the attention of the world and has
been sown into new, young ministries to the poor, for justice, to children at risk,[2] to the starving and the hungry and
the orphans of this world. The cry goes up: where are the
Wilberforces, where are the Shaftesburys who will put an
end to world hunger, that so achievable goal, in our generation? We might add: where are those who will give their
lives to the care of our earth and to halting the ecological
suicide of our planet? Thankfully, they too are emerging.[3]

But where are the witnesses/prepared-to-be-martyrs?

This is a trumpet call to the Church today, in the light of a world situation where suicide bombing is a near daily reality coming closer as people look for a faith for which some may be prepared even to die.

So who are the martyrs from the past who can instruct and inspire? They are legion. They are a cloud of witnesses. 'I do not have time to tell' of them all.[4] Indeed, if we told all the stories of those who have suffered unto death as part of the body of Christ, even if we could assemble them all, 'I suppose that even the whole world would not have room for the books that would be written'.[5]

I have chosen just a very few: from the apostolic era, the apostles Peter and Paul, and from the time of the Fathers of the Church, Polycarp, who was a disciple of John and held conversations with many who had seen Christ, and so represents an unbroken link to the teachings of Jesus. In AD 156 he is taken as a frail, elderly man but cannot deny the Christ who saved him. He is burnt at the stake as so many have been since. St John Chrysostom, the 'golden tongued', does not shrink from death which came through cruel exile so much sooner than it should have.

John Wycliffe and William Tyndale should be household names for Christians and yet they are largely forgotten or ignored today. Though 150 years separates them, they are a partnership of two people persecuted for the unglamorous linguistic labour of simply translating the Bible into English. Wycliffe, called the Morning Star of the Reformation, was by the end of his life stripped of office (he had been Professor of Divinity at Oxford) and died more or less under house arrest for the crime of translating the Bible into English. It is hard for us to imagine the hatred and invective hurled against them. According to Sir Thomas More, William Tyndale was 'a hell-hound in the kennel of the devil . . . discharging a filthy foam of blasphemies out of his brutish mouth'. Tyndale went to the stake in Holland, having by his saintly, patient attitude, like Paul before him and Brother Yun after him, brought the entire household of his jailers to faith in Christ.

From the same period, Thomas Cranmer and Hugh Latimer speak to us like heralds with a message like a cry from 'another country'. Born the son of a poor farmer in Leicester, Latimer's language was capable, like William Tyndale's before him, of speaking directly to the heart of the ploughboy with detonating effect. He was an electrifying preacher, explaining the call of Christ in a way that swept away all the encrustations of the centuries. For the first time, light was shed on the atonement as the all-important event of history and gospel preaching has kept this emphasis ever since. We need today a baptism in the courage that these men had.

Not that they were perfect. It is in a way encouraging that Cranmer in fact signed with his right hand a denial of his Protestantism under threat of torture, before 'recanting his recantation' to the consternation of his accusers. This is why he was heard to sigh, 'This unworthy right hand. . .' as he held it steadfastly over the flames that it might burn first.

As we consider these altars of our history, we are on holy ground. I pray that this memorial may serve to awaken again zeal for the knowledge and the right preaching of the good news in our land.

From the nineteenth century, James Hannington's portrait is in the stained-glass window of the church I serve in

Oxford. He responded to a call from the king of Uganda to bring some light to a place of 'total darkness'. He is one of many of his time in the great missionary movements of the nineteenth century who gave up their lives in response to the command to go into all the world and preach the gospel. Ambushed and killed on the edge of Uganda, he has served as an inspiration to a whole generation both in England and in Uganda. Later on in Uganda the Namagongo martyrs, some in their teens, in scenes of prophetic power, refused to submit to their king's advances. They imitated Hannington's example and from the seed of their sacrifice eventually grew the East Africa Revival. From this in turn came the bravery of Archbishop Janani Luwum, who stood firm in the face of Idi Amin's oppressive anti-Christian regime.

Luwum is remembered alongside Dietrich Bonhoeffer in the ten statues of twentieth-century martyrs over the West Door of Westminster Abbey. Bonhoeffer chose to return to Nazi Germany and resist even unto death, believing as he did that the victory of Nazism in Europe would destroy Christian civilisation. His message of *The Cost of Disipleship* is what this book is all about. But his excellent book *On Community* showed his and many of these martyrs' grasp of the vital link between courage and community. This book is written not simply to stimulate individuals, but in order that 'martyr-communities' be established, if such a thing is possible. For many of these martyrs, like Bonhoeffer, are also passionate about the Church. May these stories help us to create a new kind of community, where the whole body understands the need for passion and courageous living in the Church. May these churches prepare the way for the Second Coming of Jesus, in the same way that John the

Baptist prepared for his first coming. John lost his life for this cause and, if necessary, so may we.

Our final 'witnesses' will be Christians who gave their lives in China, as well as martyrs under Islamic skies. Among them is the evangelist Brother Yun, known as the 'Heavenly Man'. Yun risked death on several occasions in China and then in prison in Myanmar (Burma). He can speak to us of attitudes which for us seem revolutionary, but which are pretty commonplace in a land of persecution. His message to the Western world and to the world of those persecuted in Islamic countries has to do with consecration, being set apart for God. There is a knowledge of, a hope in and an implicit trust in God which I believe we need to catch in order to even keep the faith in the years ahead, let alone to lead our nation back to Christ.

Then, having walked with these men, we will pull together the thread of a common call to new, sacrificial levels of love for God and love for the world. Someone has said that 'business-as-usual-Christianity' will not be able to stand in the evil day that we are entering as nations abandon their Christian heritage and the church in the West enters times of turbulence. This book is a devout call to a deeper, abandoned life. It is a call for more. It is a call to 'throw off and run', as the book of Hebrews says: 'Since we are surrounded by such a great cloud of witnesses, let us throw off everything that hinders . . . and let us run with perseverance the race marked out for us' (Heb. 12:1). I invite you to get running.

# 2

# *Martyrdom or Suicide?*

*'For if all were martyrs, that die for their religion, then many heresies both contrary among themselves, and repugnant to the evident doctrine of Christ, should be truths, which is impossible.' Robert Southwell*[1]

Since the 11th September 2001, the world has changed. Some may claim this to be a Western view. But nevertheless two things happened on that day which have affected everyone directly or indirectly in this global village. One is that the world's most powerful nation declared itself to be at war. This is dangerous for everyone. It has been engaged in that 'war against terror' ever since. The second is that there has been a shift in the level of violence and terror coming upon the world. A 'new level' of world violence has been unleashed, and its most obvious agent is the suicide bomber. This has at the same time awoken many to the reality of the push from radical Islam to take territory throughout the world. We are living in times of a new crusade. The Madrid and 7/7London bombings confirm this. Following 7/7, knowing that nearly all

British Muslims condemn the attacks, Christian leaders flocked to insist that 'this has nothing to do with the real Islam'. But in fact many Muslims in the Middle East are taught that their faith does lead to 'jihad'. At the least it is a problem of interpretation of the Qur'an: study and dialogue are needed to reach a consensus on what Islam actually teaches. We are living in times when the West is under fire. But her reaction must not be a reaction in kind, a reaction of war. My contention is that what is needed is a resurrection of the spirit of the witnesses/ martyrs. I believe God wants to call forth the truth of the martyrs and the courage of the martyrs and the sacrificial love of the martyrs. Mel Gibson said that his motive for making the film *The Passion of the Christ* was that there should be what he called 'an unforgetting'. An 'unforgetting' of the agony and sacrificial love of Christ. He made a three-hour film of remembering. In the same way, this book is an unforgetting. It is a remembering of stories that can so easily be forgotten from generation to generation. And in our generation, because of our current counterfeit context, such a remembering is particularly necessary.

Thus it is appropriate for the purposes of this book to draw some distinctions between the martyr/witness and the suicide bomber/terrorist. This is not in order to provoke a racial or religious hatred – God forbid – but so that the truth be told in a contemporary way. What is needed in fact is not hatred, but love: a tidal wave of sacrificial, befriending, servant love to Islamic communities throughout the world.

I draw this distinction: that the martyr/witness goes to his or her death alone. He does not and will not take any with him. He does not desire the death of others. His is a passive submission to persecution. Essentially, he does not blow himself up, but is blown up, sometimes literally, by others. In the time of the Reformation, those who went to the stake like Ridley in Oxford might in fact have been put out of their burning misery by a necklace of gunpowder that had been placed out of mercy, if mercy it can be called, around their shoulders.

It is interesting that in the Reformation, indeed at the burning of Latimer and Ridley in Oxford in 1555, those being burnt were sometimes accused of being 'suicides'. In a three-hour sermon which Ridley and Latimer had to listen to just before the fires were lit under them, Oxford theologian Dr Richard Smith insisted that these were not martyrs like those burnt in Rome under Nero. They were not dying for truth, but for heresy. They knew their lives would have been spared had they recanted. In refusing to recant, they had in fact committed the sin of suicide.[2]

But the testimony of history is different. The plain truth is that these were men who had been forcibly arrested and taken against their will to a place where they were put to death with instruments others had prepared. When they died, no 'innocent party' perished with them.

By contrast, much has been written about the mentality of the suicide bomber or aircraft hijacker. Certainly there is courage and sacrifice of life that a higher cause inspired. Certainly there is a reaction to perceived oppression at the hands of those targeted. There may well be a repaying of perceived terror or war prosecuted by the targeted country, for example the USA, UK or Russia.

But the vital distinction is that there is also carnage,

bloodshed and wreckage caused. There is bereavement, unpitying contempt and the terror of the victims. There is the active desire to take others to death, without which the act would lose meaning. Finally, there is the pulling of the trigger, the extracting of the pin, the connecting of the wires, the call made to the mobile phone executed by the suicide. It is instigated and timed by the bomber. There is an utter and complete separation between the structure of the two acts. This may appear a truism, but I underline it lest some deconstructionist set about the sorry labour of amalgamating the two entirely separate acts of the martyr/witness and the suicide bomber/terrorist. They look similar in some ways: rather like a counterfeit, in fact. But counterfeit is precisely what it is, and we need, if I may say it, the courage to say so.

It is conceivable that a better comparison would be between the suicide bomber and the soldier. And yet in this case, the purposeful targeting of civilians places the suicide bomber in a category of destruction that is quite distinct and, in my opinion, devilish.

It is interesting that the apostle Paul, anticipating his own death perhaps, provided a further and final distinction:

> If I give all I possess to the poor and surrender my body to the flames, but have not love, I gain nothing. Love . . . keeps no record of wrongs. Love . . . always protects, always trusts, always hopes, always perseveres. (1 Cor. 13:3–7)

I guess this is the ultimate test of all action, and the test of this book. I hope with it to kindle courage, but at the same time to kindle love. The martyrs/witnesses to whom we now turn are those who have been imitators of Christ.

Forcibly taken and falsely accused, they have not lost courage. They have spread the love of God in the world. They have not crashed into others exploding the life out of them. They have offered life to all they met. My hope is that through these pages they would keep on offering life, not death, and love, not war, today.

To return to the starting point of this chapter, I am told that since 9/11 around 34,000 Americans have converted to Islam.[3] Time will tell whether the 7/7 bombing in London will have a similar impact. When asked why that act of terror and carnage should attract rather than repel, Dutch peace worker Brother Andrew says, 'Many today want to believe in something that people are willing to die for.' When asked by his friends in terrorist organisations like Hamas to explain the heart of Christianity, he sometimes thinks, 'You Muslims will never know what the true meaning of the cross is until we Christians have started to live out what Jesus meant when he said to give up everything we have for you. How can I be Jesus to the terrorist? I am only Jesus to him when I will die for him.'

'Instead,' he reflects ruefully, 'we bomb them, annihilate them, imprison them. We will do almost anything but go to the enemy in the streets who is building a ghetto, building a mosque, because no one will go and befriend their enemy.'[4]

And yet this, if we can but call it to mind, is what the martyrs/witnesses have always been doing: leaving their comfort zone; going and loving and speaking and imitating Christ in the most inhospitable territory. We turn now to the task of unforgetting them.

# 3

# *Paul and Peter*

*'God has honoured him in allowing him to suffer. The New Testament speaks of this honour of suffering. It is not for nothing. It is a signpost, pointing up higher, where honour is given and the crown of life is received.' Karl Barth*[1]

Peter and Paul were martyred in Rome on the same day, so tradition has it.[2] One was crucified upside down and one was beheaded. What had happened to cause such steadfastness? And what had they said to provoke such decisive opposition?

According to Clement of Rome, 'Paul displayed the prize of endurance: seven times in bonds, driven to exile, stoned, appearing as a herald in both East and the West, he . . . taught righteousness to the whole world, and after reaching the limits of the West bore witness before the rulers . . . Then he passed from the world. . .'[3]

The lives of Peter and Paul and their message remain utterly remarkable and continue to echo hauntingly into today's generation, who long to be worthy followers of Christ.

From the moment that the 'remarkable gaze'[4] of Christ settled on him, Simon knew that he was shifted somehow into a heavenly destiny. Perhaps his roots in this earth were loosened on that very first day, when Christ 'looked at him' and changed his name from Simon to Peter, the rock.

A similar thing happens to Saul when on the road to prosecute his bloody business of 'murderous threats' against the Christians. He has a heavenly vision by which he is gripped and he cannot from then on be disobedient. He too finds his old allegiances have been cut, in a moment. He aspires to heaven and to please and preach Christ whom he has been persecuting. He has in common with Peter that his name is changed, and that he keeps on telling the truth about Christ, unbearably courageously, wherever he goes.

Their message and example can grip us still. They whisper in the background, as it were, to encourage so many witnesses/martyrs today. My prayer is that they speak to the West to arise with courage in the same way that they speak to the East. I remember being in a restaurant with Brother Yun in Oxford and his translator telling me that if it had been a Chinese restaurant, Yun would simply have spent the entire time we were there evangelising the kitchen staff. In the same way, Paul evangelised the prison staff in his day, and so, when he was in prison, did Yun. Let us dig in to see what is this 'apostolic courage' so needed today.

### Apostolic courage

Paul seems to have moved from one world to another during the days of his conversion. It is interesting that Ananias who is sent to baptise Paul is told that Paul is a 'chosen instrument to carry my name before the Gentiles and their kings and before the people of Israel', but also that 'I will show him how much he must suffer for my name' (Acts 9:15–16). So from day one of his Christian life, he was preaching in the Damascus synagogues and 'baffled the Jews . . . by proving that Jesus is the Christ' (Acts 9:22). Immediately he is at risk of death and has to be let out of the city in a basket lowered through an opening in the city wall. So ends his first preaching. Paul's persecution, closeness to death and courage to continue are present from the beginning. He similarly preaches in Jerusalem and talks and debates with Grecian Jews. But again they try to kill him. The words used of Paul are 'fearlessly' and 'boldly'. Somehow, Paul gets into the habit of anticipating persecution and suffering in a way that is almost totally foreign to the church today in the West. Perhaps it is the word from Ananias about 'how much he must suffer' that lifts him out of the self-pity or self-doubt others experience. It is clear that self-preservation or avoiding trouble is not his concern. He tells the Ephesian leaders, 'I only know that in every city the Holy Spirit warns me that prison and hardships are facing me' (Acts 20:23). When Agabus wants to prophesy him out of going to Jerusalem, he rebukes him: 'Why are you weeping and breaking my heart? I am ready not only to be bound, but also to die . . . for the name of the Lord Jesus' (Acts 21:13).

Peter was just as fearless, after he had encountered Jesus risen from the dead. Perhaps it was the grip of those words of Christ talking of his destiny to tend to lambs, feed sheep, care for the flock. Perhaps it was the knowledge from Christ that 'when you are old you will stretch out your hands, and someone else will dress you and lead you where you do not want to go' (John 21:18). Perhaps it was the power of Pentecost. Whatever it was, Peter changed dramatically from the one who fled at Christ's arrest. He was the first to suffer for the message of Christ, when he was arrested, imprisoned and threatened. Some days later he was whipped for his courageous proclaiming of the message of Christ. His reaction was not to be silenced but to call a room-shaking prayer meeting and ask heaven that they might speak with even more boldness and that signs and wonders would break out in Jerusalem. Later, as a result of a dream, he broke out of the Jewish world, and was responsible for turning the Church towards the nations. But within months he was in prison again at the hands of Herod.

Peter's words are remarkable when he is confronted and they are a lesson to us in these days of political correctness and a Church which is so often intimidated into silence. He says, 'Judge for yourselves whether it is right in God's sight to obey you rather than God. For we cannot help speaking about what we have seen and heard' (Acts 4:19–20). Here is the definition of a witness: someone who has seen and probably heard, and who will not be silent. Later, when arrested again, Peter repeats, 'We must obey God rather than men!' (Acts 5:29) – even though this provokes the Sadducees to want to put him to death.

### Apostolic comfort

Paul and Peter both developed a message for those who were to suffer for Christ that speaks comfortable words today.

In the end Peter will be put to death by being crucified

upside down in Rome. On the way there he writes letters of comfort, of which two have survived. He urges his followers 'as aliens and strangers in the world' (1 Pet. 2:11). He speaks of 'an inheritance that can never perish, spoil or fade – kept in heaven for you' (1 Pet. 1:4). He talks of suffering for doing good and enduring it, adding, 'To this you were called, because Christ suffered for you' (1 Pet. 2:21). He talks of not being surprised, but rejoicing in the fiery trial happening to them. Provided they are not suffering for doing wrong, but are suffering for being Christians, like Paul he sees this as 'participating in the sufferings of Christ' (1 Pet. 4:13) and being blessed because of this. It is a time when 'the Spirit of glory and of God rests on you' (1 Pet. 4:14). Peter thinks back to his own 'heavenly vision', the transfiguration, in his second letter, saying, 'We ourselves heard this voice that came from heaven when we were with him on the sacred mountain' (2 Pet. 1:18). He was an 'eye-witness of his majesty' and maybe this is why, in the end, he will be a witness/martyr.

The Second Letter to the Corinthians is for Paul the place above all where this comfort is expressed to those into whose lives the sufferings of Christ flow. Here we have the praise given to the God of all comfort, who comforts us in our troubles so that we may comfort others with the comfort we ourselves have received from God. Here we have the mysterious claim that the sufferings of Christ flow over into our lives, rather like the teaching that Paul is filling up in his flesh 'what is still lacking in regard to Christ's afflictions' (Col. 1:24). This is speaking not of the atoning sufferings of Christ, but of the suffering he experiences as his body, the Church, is persecuted. 'Saul, Saul, why do you persecute me?' (Acts 9:4) was the phrase Paul had heard at the moment of his conversion.

To the Corinthians, Paul talks about being 'under great pressure, far beyond our ability to endure' (2 Cor. 1:8). He says he has 'despaired even of life [and] felt the sentence of death'. But when he does, it is to discover how to cling to Christ. He calls us to rely 'not . . . on ourselves but on God, who raises the dead' (2 Cor. 1:8–9). He has been 'hard pressed on every side, but not crushed; perplexed, but not in despair; persecuted, but not abandoned; struck down, but not destroyed' (2 Cor. 4:8–9). He knew the literal meaning of all this, and adds that he is always carrying around in his body 'the death of Jesus'. He calls his listeners through all this to see the life of Jesus revealed through our mortal bodies. It is the deep way of Christ that Paul is calling us to: the 'now and not yet' of the kingdom of God; the suffering triumph of the resurrection; the victory through defeat of the one who wins by losing his life. Paul sums it up: 'through glory and dishonour, bad report and good report; genuine, yet regarded as impostors; known, yet regarded as unknown; dying, and yet we live on; beaten, and yet not killed; sorrowful, yet always rejoicing; poor, yet making many rich; having nothing, and yet possessing everything' (2 Cor. 6:8–10).

What is comforting is the heavenly perspective. And this is the comfort of all the martyrs: it is a vision of heaven. With heavy irony, we reflect that Stephen the first martyr cried out as they began to stone him, 'I see heaven open and the Son of Man standing at the right hand of God' (Acts 7:56) – and the cloaks of those who stoned him were laid down at the feet of a young man, Saul, who was consenting to his death. That young man, as he grew older, knew that Stephen had been right. And he grew to sustain himself on his own vision from heaven, a perspective that enabled him to bring comfort from heaven to all the generations that have followed.

## Apostolic message

The apostolic message of Peter and of Paul is one we do well to tuck into our hearts and meditate on deeply so as to bring it out in a language our contemporaries can catch hold of. The trigger for the message is that they are witnesses,[5] as we have seen. They are witnesses to the fact of Christ being the one who towers over history. He is the one from whom history flows and to whom it is going. The way into this message varies for them, depending on who they are talking to. Paul is different in Athens and Antioch, and Peter is different in Jerusalem on the Day of Pentecost when he refers to the prophet Joel, and in Caesarea when he jumps off from a starting point of John's baptism.

The message bears analysis: Paul and Peter speak to Jewish audiences, and they both speak to non-Jewish listeners on different occasions. But the common words and the common burden are clear: the message is about the goodness, the saving aroma and the decisive acts of the person of Christ. As Peter says, 'Jesus of Nazareth was a man accredited by God to you by miracles, wonders and signs, which God did among you through him, as you yourselves know' (Acts 2:22). He talks of 'how God anointed [him] with the Holy Spirit and power, and how he went around doing good and healing' (Acts 10:38).

Paul talks more of his own encounter and meeting with the risen Christ and his fulfilling of Scripture. They both tell the story of Christ's death on the cross and rising again and being appointed judge of all. This is the true revolution of the message and why it has caused a separation in all cultures and throughout history. Then they call their listeners to come under his rule, to repent and change and become his followers, to receive forgiveness and the refreshing of the Holy Spirit. They call their generation and all generations to enter a completely new kingdom: the kingdom of God. This is dynamite and still is today, as it casts the long shadow of a question mark over all the tired ways of the world that have been tried and found wanting. Christ is still calling today and this book is an incitement to get filled with his message; to get filled with courage to proclaim it urgently to the ends of our culture with passionate love and comfort.

Attempting to encompass this, one writer says that Paul transformed the proclamation of God's kingdom to the 'lost sheep of the house of Israel' into a world movement. Despite all handicaps, Paul judged precisely the prevailing mood. He offered a religion sufficient to attract those on the outer fringes of synagogue worship and even beyond. 'The ideal of community in which there was neither bond nor free, Jew nor Greek, but which was united in love of a Saviour and freed thereby from the Law, the power of fate, and the malevolent astral lords of time could also become the ideal of many of the inhabitants of the Greco Roman world.'[6] The Saviour Paul preached was not a saviour god of current pagan myth but a historical figure who was fully God and fully man. Paul had found that in Christ some of the most powerful forces of life in the Empire were brought together. He also encountered forces almost equally powerful. The Jewish orthodoxy on one hand and the imperial cult on the other were a combined firepower that was already leading to the inevitable creation of a string of martyrs who included all the apostles bar one. Yet their courage was and is inspiration and light to the world.

## Fifteen apostolic examples

In the end, these two apostles gave up their lives for this cause. They did so along with all the other apostles. *Foxe's Book of Martyrs*[7] records the following stories which some question but other historians, despite the hagiographical tone, affirm.

James was the elder brother of John, and a relative of Christ. 'As James was led to the place of martyrdom, his accuser was brought to repent of his conduct by the apostle's extraordinary courage and undauntedness, and fell down at his feet to request his pardon, professing himself a Christian, and resolving that James should not receive the crown of martyrdom alone. Hence they were both beheaded at the same time in AD 44.'

Philip worked in Upper Asia, and was martyred at Heliopolis, in Phrygia. 'He was scourged, thrown into prison, and afterwards crucified, in AD 54.'

Matthew the tax collector 'was born at Nazareth. He wrote his gospel in Hebrew, which was afterwards translated into Greek by James the Less. He worked in Parthia, and Ethiopia, in which latter country he suffered martyrdom, being slain with a halberd in the city of Nadabah, AD 60.'

James the Less was elected to the oversight of the churches of Jerusalem, and was the author of the book of James. 'At the age of ninety-four he was beaten and stoned by the Jews; and finally had his brains dashed out with a club.'

Matthias was elected to fill the vacant place of Judas. 'He was stoned at Jerusalem and then beheaded.'

Andrew, the brother of Peter, 'preached the gospel to many Asiatic nations; but on his arrival at Edessa he was taken and crucified on a cross, the two ends of which were fixed transversely in the ground. Hence the derivation of the term, St Andrew's Cross.'

Mark was born of Jewish parents of the tribe of Levi. He is supposed to have been converted to Christianity by Peter, under whose inspection he wrote his Gospel in the Greek language. 'Mark was dragged to pieces by the people of Alexandria, at Serapis their idol, ending his life under their merciless hands.'

Peter, among many others, was condemned to death and crucified in Rome. 'Nero sought matter against Peter to put him to death; which, when the people perceived, they entreated Peter with much ado that he would fly the city. On leaving Rome, Peter had a vision of Christ entering the city. Peter said, "Lord, whither dost Thou go?" To whom He answered and said, "I am come again to be crucified." By this, Peter, perceiving his suffering to be understood, returned into the city. Jerome says that he was crucified, his head being down and his feet upward, himself so requiring, because he was (he said) unworthy to be crucified after the same form and manner as the Lord was.'

Paul the apostle, who before was called Saul, 'after his

great travail and unspeakable labours in promoting the Gospel of Christ, suffered also in this first persecution under Nero. Nero sent two of his soldiers, Ferega and Parthemius, to bring him word of his death. They, coming to Paul instructing the people, desired him to pray for them, that they might believe; who told them that shortly after they should believe and be baptised at His tomb. This done, the soldiers came and led him out of the city to the place of execution, where he, after his prayers made, gave his neck to the sword.'

Jude, the brother of James, was crucified at Edessa in AD 72.

Bartholomew was an apostle to India. 'He was at length cruelly beaten and then crucified by the impatient idolaters.'

Thomas, called Didymus, 'preached the Gospel in Parthia and India, where exciting the rage of the pagan priests, he was martyred by being thrust through with a spear'.

Luke, the evangelist, travelled with Paul through various countries, and is supposed to have been hanged on an olive tree, by the priests of Greece.

Simon, surnamed Zelotes, 'preached the Gospel in Mauritania, Africa, and even in Britain, in which latter country he was crucified, AD 74'.

John, 'the "beloved disciple", founded the churches of Smyrna, Pergamos, Sardis, Philadelphia, Laodicea and Thyatira. From Ephesus he was ordered to be sent to Rome, where he was cast into a cauldron of boiling oil. He escaped by miracle, without injury. Domitian afterwards banished him to the Isle of Patmos, where he wrote the book of Revelation. Nerva recalled him. He was the only apostle who escaped a violent death.'

This catalogue is inspiring and should be held with a certain awe by Christians today. It is intriguing that one of the songs sung in China, as reported by Brother Yun, catalogues these examples. I don't include it here as an example of great poetry, but to suggest that these stories are motivational for a church under fire like that in China. And they can be for us in the West.

From the time the church was birthed on the day of Pentecost
The followers of the Lord have willingly sacrificed themselves.
Tens of thousands have died that the gospel might prosper.
As such they have obtained the crown of life.

*Chorus*
To be a martyr for the Lord, to be a martyr for the Lord,
I am willing to die gloriously for the Lord.

Those apostles who love the Lord to the end
Willingly followed the Lord down the path of suffering.
John was exiled to the lonely isle of Patmos.
Stephen was stoned to death by an angry crowd.

Matthew was stabbed to death in Persia by a mob.
Mark died as horses pulled his two legs apart.
Doctor Luke was cruelly hanged.
Peter, Philip and Simon were crucified on a cross.

Bartholomew was skinned alive by the heathen.
Thomas died in India as five horses pulled his body apart.
The apostle James was beheaded by King Herod.
Little James was cut in half by a sharp saw.

James the brother of the Lord was stoned to death.
Judas was tied to a pillar and shot by arrows.
Matthias had his head cut off in Jerusalem.
Paul was a martyr under Nero.

I am willing to take up the cross and go forward,
To follow the apostles down the road of sacrifice,
That tens of thousands of precious souls can be saved.
I am willing to leave all and be a martyr for the Lord.[8]

Although the fates of Bartholomew, James the Less and Thomas appear to differ from Foxe's account, the fact of the courage of the early Church is one of the vital motivators for withstanding persecution in the underground church in China. Would that it might be an incitement to courage equally in the church in the West. Foxe concludes, 'Yet, notwithstanding all these continual persecutions and horrible punishments, the Church daily increased, deeply rooted in the doctrine of the apostles and of men apostolical, and watered plenteously with the blood of saints.'

# 4

# *Polycarp and Chrysostom*

*'The acts of the early Christian martyrs are full of evidence which shows how Christ transfigures for his own the hour of their agony by granting them the unspeakable assurance of his presence. In the hour of cruellest suffering they bear for his sake, they are made partakers in the perfect joy and bliss of fellowship with him.' Dietrich Bonhoeffer*[1]

Under the Roman Empire until Constantine's conversion in 312, to become a Christian meant being in danger of death. The word 'witness' still meant also 'martyr'. Eusebius, Tacitus, Suetonius, Clement of Rome and other early letter writers tell tales of martyrdom and courage. Tertullian begins to reflect on the persecutions, for example on the paradox that criminals when arrested denied and hid their crimes, whereas for Christians, 'Not a man is ashamed of it. Not a man regrets – unless indeed that he was not a Christian earlier . . . What sort of evil is it that has none of the native marks of evil (fear, shame, shuffling, regret, lament)? What? Is it evil when the criminal is glad, where accusation is the thing he prays for and punishment is his felicity?'[2]

The main reason for the persecution was twofold. First there was the affront to the authority of Caesar, the temporal ruler. In a totalitarian world a 'separated group' was an offence. Then there was the spiritual affront to deeply embedded spiritual authorities and powers which ideas of the uniqueness and authority of Christ represent. This was and remains a double cocktail that can lead to violence against Christians in any society. This was or is the motive for massacre in France under Louis XIV, in England under Mary, in China under Mao and his inheritors, and in many Muslim countries today. But in Roman times, the belief was also that the presence of Christians brought the anger of the gods on the world. Tertullian in a famous passage begins to tease the authorities: 'If the Tiber reaches the walls, if the Nile does not rise to the fields, if the sky doesn't move or the earth does, the cry is at once: "The Christians to the lion!" What, all of them to one lion?'[3]

According to Foxe, these waves of persecution lasted, under the emperors Nero, Domitian, Trajan, Marcus Aurelius, Severus, Maximus, Decius, Valerian, Aurelian and Diocletian, from AD 67 till 312. There were ten waves in all, sometimes seemingly random, and depending on the whim of a man. There were some examples, of course, of people being intimidated out of their faith, for example in Carthage.[4] Nevertheless, it revealed a never weakening courage and strong hold on Christ on the part of Christians whether in Italy, France, Germany, Britain or North Africa, indeed throughout the Empire, for the faith had taken root everywhere.

## Polycarp

One of the most memorable examples is Polycarp. He was a disciple of John who held conversations with many who had seen Christ, and so represents an unbroken link to the teachings of Jesus. He became Bishop of Smyrna (now Izmir, Turkey), just north of Ephesus, and was Irenaeus's teacher. His letter to the Philippians is a powerful guide to the character of faith in Christ which in the end Polycarp was called on to live out. Persecution broke out in Smyrna and Polycarp was persuaded to escape to a farm, where he began to pray for those caught in the persecution as well as for the 'Church throughout all the world'. It is said that on that night three days before his arrest, he had a dream in which he saw his pillow on fire. When he woke up he told his friends that 'I must needs be burned alive'[5]. Eventually discovered, he invited the soldiers to sit down to a meal and asked their permission to pray for an hour. 'On their granting this he stood up, being so full of the grace of God, that for the space of two hours he could not hold his peace, and the hearers were astonished and many sorry they had come after so venerable an old man.' This gives a rare window of information on the prayer practice of the early Church: out loud, unceasing, believing, prevailing prayer which had its effect.

On the way to execution, he was met by the chief constable, who took him into his carriage and tried to persuade him: 'What harm is there to say Caesar is Lord and to sacrifice?'

After a pause, Polycarp replied, 'I do not intend to do what you advise me.'

Then the mood changed and the Father of the Church and friend of the companion of Christ was pushed down, injured his leg and was sworn at terribly. As he walked to the stadium, where the noise was deafening, there occurred this memorable event: a voice from heaven 'heard by those of our friends who were present' said, 'Be strong, Polycarp, and play the man.' No one saw the speaker, but the voice was heard and noted . . . and remembered 1,500 years later when another bishop in another country, Bishop Latimer in Oxford, would encourage Master Ridley with the same words as they faced the fires together.

Polycarp is again pressed by the proconsul to 'have respect to his old age' and deny his faith and avoid the flames. He then replies, in words that ring out like a trumpet to our times, 'Eighty-six years have I served him, and he has done me no wrong. How then can I blaspheme my King who saved me?'

The proconsul then says, 'I have wild beasts.'

'Bid them be brought.'

'If you despise the beasts, unless you change your mind I shall have you burnt.'

'You threaten me with the fire that burns for an hour, and after a little while is quenched; for you are ignorant of the fire of judgement to come, and of the everlasting punishment reserved for the ungodly. But why delay? Do as you wish.'

At this the herald announces to the crowd the result of the interrogation: Polycarp has confessed himself to be a Christian. The reaction of the crowd in great clamour is to call for the lion or for the burning of one who is 'the father of the Christians and the destroyer of our gods'. And so with great speed the mob assembles logs and faggots. Polycarp, old and grey-haired, removes his outer garments, and at the point of being nailed to the stake has the authority still to say, 'Let me be as I am. He that gives me power to abide the fire will help me too without being nailed to it, to stay at the pyre unflinching.'

Polycarp then begins to pray a remarkable prayer, looking up to heaven like Stephen: 'I bless you God Almighty, Father of your beloved and blessed child Jesus Christ . . . God of angels and Powers and all creation and the whole race of the righteous who live before your face, I bless you . . . that I may take a portion among the martyrs in the cup of Christ . . . May I today be welcome before your face as a rich and acceptable sacrifice . . . For this reason I praise you through Christ. . .'

Then the fire is lit, but engulfs everything except the body of Polycarp. And here occurs one of those mysteries which we are tempted to dismiss as unreal embellishing, and yet it is echoed in many accounts of the martyrs, whether in England under Mary or in Uganda at Namagongo. We read in the eyewitness account: 'The fire made the appearance of a vaulted roof, like a ship's sail filling out with the wind. There it was in the midst, not like flesh burning, but like a loaf baking, or like gold and silver being refined in the furnace. Moreover we caught a fragrance as of the breath of frankincense or some other precious spice.' An executioner stabbed Polycarp with a dagger, 'and there came out a dove and so much blood as put out the fire and all the multitude marvelled'.

This event of AD 156 acted as an incentive for bravery and fidelity and still does today. It was shortly followed by other acts of courage in France. In Lyons, on the 1st August AD 177, among 48 Christians killed in prison or the amphitheatre were Sanctus, Maturus, Attalus and Blandina, a servant girl who went through torture and endured longer than any, all the while encouraging others.[6] With them was Pothinus, the elderly but courageous Bishop of Lyons of whom Eusebius says, 'The blessed Pothinus was 90 years of age, and very weak in body. But the earnest desire for martyrdom filled him with that renewed strength which a willing spirit supplies. He gave the good witness and received blows of every kind heaped on him by hands and feet regardless of age. Scarcely breathing he was cast into prison where after two days he gave up the ghost.'[7]

Throughout the time of the Church Fathers, through to the conversion of Constantine, to use Tertullian's phrase, 'the blood of the martyrs became the seed of the Church'.

## St John Chrysostom

Chrysostom converted as an adult from his brilliant career as a rhetorician and lawyer. He preached in fourth-century Antioch and from 398 to 404 in Constantinople so compellingly that he was called the prince of preachers. In the same year that Augustine was baptised by Ambrose in Milan, Chrysostom preached his most famous sermons. In Antioch a revolt against taxes had led to the imperial images being defaced. This was a formal rebellion against the supreme authority on earth. Realising the peril in which they found themselves, the people of the city repented and awaited imperial wrath. Would the city be sacked, as was quite possible? Would there be indiscriminate arrests and people thrown to the sword, beasts or the stake? During this time, John won the hearts of the people to Christ through his series of sermons 'On the Statues', in which he likened the fear of imperial wrath at the defaming of the imperial statues to the need to be reconciled to God through Christ. His message was given, like Spurgeon 1,700 years later, with the Bible open in one hand and the equivalent of the newspapers in the other. Here is some of it:

> Assuredly you gather from this the mercy of God: how unspeakable, how boundless, how transcending all description! Here (in the affair of the statues) the person insulted is of the same nature, only once in his lifetime has he experienced this; and then it was not done to his face; nor while he was present to see it or hear it.
>
> But with regard to God . . . throughout every day he is insulted, although present and seeing and hearing it, and yet he sends not forth his lightning, nor the sea does he command to overflow, nor does he bid the earth to cleave asunder; but he forbears, he suffers long, and still offers to pardon those who have insulted him. 'Who can utter the mighty acts of the Lord? Who can show forth all his praise?'
>
> How many have not only cast down but also trodden under foot the image of God? For when you throttle a debtor, when you strip him, when you drag him away, you trample under foot God's image . . . Hear Paul saying: 'a man . . . is the image and Glory of God'; and again let us hear God himself saying: 'Let us make man in our own image. . .'
>
> May there be then some favourable and propitious change! This certainly I foretell and testify, that though this cloud (the threat following the desecration of the statues) should pass away, and yet you remain in the same state of listlessness, we shall have to suffer much heavier evils than we are now

dreading. For I do not fear as much the wrath of the emperor as your own listlessness. Surely it is not sufficient that we supplicate two or three days, but it is necessary that we make a change in our whole life.

In compelling and irresistible words, Chrysostom at the same time calls his people to prayer and introduces his call to them to fast:

Let us not then despair of our safety, but let us pray; let us make invocation; let us supplicate; let us send embassy to the King that is above with many tears. We have too in this fast, an ally, an assistant to good intercession . . . Therefore as when the winter is over, the sailor draws his ship to the deep; and the soldier burnishes his arms and makes ready for battle; the farmer sharpens his sickle; the traveller boldly undertakes long journeys and the wrestler bares himself for the contest. So too, when the fast makes his appearance . . . let us strip for the contest . . . Put on your spiritual armour and you have become a soldier. Strip yourself of worldly thought. The season is one of wrestling . . . Cultivate thy soul; cut away the thorns. I speak not indeed of such a fast as many keep, but of real fasting. Not merely abstinence from meats, but of sins. . .

What was it that delivered (the Ninevites) from such inevitable wrath . . . Was it fasting only and sackcloth? We say not so: but the change of their whole life. . .

Running through John's preaching is this call to a radical change of lifestyle. With startling modernity he preaches into the dynamic of household repentance. At different points, he addresses fathers and calls them to gather their entire family together for such a time as this, as this final extract shows:

I desire to fix three precepts in your mind: to speak ill of no one; to hold no one for an enemy; and to expel from the mouth the evil custom of oaths. Let every one when he has returned home call together his wife and children, and let him say, a special tribute is called for this day, that is to say: to have no enemy, to speak ill of no man, and to swear not at all. Let us consider, let us think: how we may fulfil these precepts. Let us correct each other. If we set our lives in order, I pledge myself and promise that there will be deliverance from this present calamity. . .

This is a martyr's call to repentance in a city where 'the lively licentiousness of the Greeks blended with the hereditary softness of the Syrians: fashion was the only law and pleasure the only pursuit'.[8]

When he was forcibly elevated to the bishopric of Constantinople, Chrysostom showed what kind of lifestyle was dear to his heart. In actions which anticipate those of the saintly Bishop of Digne in Hugo's *Les Misérables*, he emptied the bishop's palace of furniture and plate and gave it to hospitals. He devoted his large income to the same purpose.

His was a downward mobility that speaks to us today in our glutted, sensual and possession-filled world. We find in these early witnesses/martyrs the threefold cord of calm courage, clear communication about Christ the Lord of all, and simple lifestyle. These aspects of Christ's character still win hearts even today. When the Archbishop of York, David Hope, announced his intention to step down and cut his salary to one fifth, he hit the front pages of every paper in the land. 'The greatest of these is Hope' announced one tabloid, showing the hunger in our land for something that resembles true discipleship.

Chrysostom made enemies by opposing the by then common practice of monks and nuns living together under the same roof. On a visit to Ephesus, he deposed six bishops for simony. But the tide of power was reacting against him and soon a pact formed between his deputy and the empress led to his violent arrest.

Chrysostom, like Latimer after him, would not compromise with the prevailing riches of the society around him. He would not be silent either. He seemed in some way to have 'left the world'. And this he had in common with the other witnesses/martyrs. Their allegiance is in another country and so they are, to a certain extent, free to communicate the values of that other kingdom. And therein lies their offence.

During this period Chrysostom uttered the memorable words:

> Riches I do not sigh for. Death I do not shrink from; and life I do not desire, save only for the progress of your souls. But you know my friends the true cause of my fall: It is that I have not lined my walls with rich tapestry; I have not clothed my self in silk; I have not flattered the effeminacy and sensuality of certain men . . . But why need I say more? Jezebel is raging and Elijah must fly; Herodias is taking her pleasure and John must be bound in chains. . .

The contemporary relevance of this cannot escape us. We need to be wooed not only by the courage and the Christ-like ethics, but also by the downward mobility and espousal of a simple lifestyle.

John had been banished already, but was reinstated by popular demand. Now he was dragged from the cathedral during a service of baptism on Easter eve 404. 'The water of regeneration was stained with blood,' writes Palladius. 'The female candidates, half dressed, were driven by licentious soldiers into the dark streets. The Eucharistic elements were profaned by pagan hands . . . Private dwellings were invaded and supporters of John were thrown into prison, whipped and tortured.'[9]

John Chrysostom was sentenced to harsh exile and forced journeyings, which were in effect a martyrdom for him. His reaction was this:

> What can I fear? Will it be death? But you know that Christ is my life and all that I shall gain by death. Will it be exile? But the earth is the Lord's. Will it be loss of wealth? But we brought nothing into the world and can carry nothing out. Thus all the terrors of the world are contemptible in my eyes. I smile at all its good things. . .

His letters from exile show that in adversity, he continued to care for the Church and look calmly forward to heaven. As a result of three months' journeying on foot in the keeping of two brutal guards, he died in Pontus in 407, his last words being, 'Glory be to God in all things.' Thirty-one years after his death, he was reburied with great pomp in Constantinople and the new emperor knelt at his coffin to ask forgiveness for the guilt of his parents and for the injustice done to this most godly man.

# 5

## Wycliffe and Tyndale

*'Men are God's method. The Church is looking for better methods; God is looking for better men. The training of the twelve was the great, difficult and enduring work of Christ . . . It is not great talents or great learning or great preachers that God needs, but men and women great in holiness, great in faith, great in courage, great for God. Men always preaching by holy sermons in the pulpit, by holy lives outside it. These can mould a generation for God.' E.M. Bounds*

We enter now the holy ground of the lives and deaths of those who gave themselves to bring the English-speaking world the message of heaven, the Bible, in its own language. They glimpsed the revelation locked up inside the Latin translation and the Greek and Hebrew Bible. Over a period of 150 years, they dared to unlock it and set the truth free, by translating it into English. In so doing, they defied the combined might of the English throne and the Roman Church, who fought them implacably every step of the way. So threatened was the status quo, the spirit and the superstition of the age, that every threat and invective was thrown at them, including the ultimate terror.

## John Wycliffe

John Wycliffe, called the Morning Star of the Reformation because of his John the Baptist-like forerunner ministry, died more or less under house arrest in 1384. Elected as Warden of Canterbury Hall, Oxford, and then to the chair of Professor of Divinity, he became convinced of the errors of the Roman Church. In public lectures 'he lashed their vices and opposed their follies. He unfolded a variety of abuses covered by the darkness of superstition . . . The usurpations of the court of Rome was a favourite topic. On these he expatiated with all the keenness of argument, joined to logical reasoning. This soon procured him the clamour of the clergy, who, with the archbishop of Canterbury, deprived him of his office.'[1] Wycliffe spoke out in his lectures against the Pope: his usurpation, his infallibility, his pride, his avarice and his tyranny. He was the first who termed the Pope Antichrist. From the Pope, he turned to the pomp, the luxury and trappings of the bishops, and compared them with the simplicity of primitive bishops. Their superstitions and deceptions were topics that he pursued with energy of mind and logical precision.

All this was a prelude to his life's work, the translation of the Bible into English, first publishing a tract showing the necessity of it. The zeal of the bishops to suppress the Scriptures greatly promoted its sale, and those who were not able to buy copies got hold of particular Gospels or epistles. Afterwards, when during the persecution of Wycliffe's followers martyrs began to be burned to death, it was common to fasten about the neck of the condemned heretic such of these scraps of Scripture as were found in his possession, which generally shared his fate.

Wycliffe ventured a step further, and began to take on the doctrine of transubstantiation. In his lecture before the University of Oxford in 1381, he attacked the doctrine, and subsequently published a treatise. The vice-chancellor of Oxford, calling together the heads of the university, condemned Wycliffe's doctrines as heretical and threatened their author with excommunication. The court condemned his teachings, some as erroneous, others as heretical. The king granted a licence to imprison him, but the Commons made the king revoke this act as illegal. The University of Oxford was ordered to search for all heresies and books published by Wycliffe, in consequence of which order the university became a scene of tumult. Wycliffe is supposed to have retired from the storm into an obscure part of the kingdom. The seeds were scattered, however, and Wycliffe's opinions were so prevalent that it was said that if you met two persons upon the road, you might be sure that one was a Lollard. This term given to Wycliffe's followers derived from the Dutch term for vagabonds – *lollen*, meaning 'to mutter'. Wycliffe repaired to his parish of Lutterworth, where he was parson, and there he died quietly.

Forty-one years later, the Bishop of Lincoln and other powerful men had his bones dug up and redressed him in clerical garb, in order for his carcass to be defrocked and then burnt to ashes and thrown into the River Swift in 1428. Foxe concludes that they were:

. . .thinking they might abolish the name of Wycliffe completely. But these and all others must know that, as there is no counsel against the Lord, so there is no keeping down of verity, but it will spring up and come out of dust and ashes, as appeared right well in this man; for though they dug up his body, burned his bones, and drowned his ashes, yet the Word of God and the truth of his doctrine, with the fruit and success thereof, they could not burn.

## William Tyndale

Tyndale was himself brought to humiliation 108 years later near Antwerp, on the 5th August 1536. In a process unchanged since the days of John Huss, he was forced to kneel in the vestments of a priest in the public square of Vilvoorde, Holland. His hands were scraped with the blade of a knife, symbolically removing the oil with which he had been anointed at his consecration. The sacraments were placed in his hands and taken away. As the cup was removed, the bishops cursed him: 'O cursed Judas, because you have abandoned the counsel of peace . . . we take away from you this cup of redemption.' Other curses were pronounced, as one by one his vestments were removed and he was reclothed as a layman. The way was now clear for the strangling and death by burning five days later of this brave man who, more than any other, fashioned the English language as we now know it. Before the flames licked around his body, he cried out with a loud voice: 'Lord! open the king of England's eyes!' Eyewitnesses spoke 'of the patient sufferance of Master Tyndale at the time of his execution'.

The king of England whose eyes were duly opened was James I, who commissioned the first official version of the Bible in English. Although Wycliffe had paved the way with his translation, when it finally emerged 75 years later the 'Authorised Version' was overwhelmingly Tyndale's. Almost any passage in the Old or New Testament that is memorable belongs to him. A 1998 study shows that 84 per cent of the New Testament and 75 per cent of the Old are his. He defied the Constitutions of Oxford and in translating the Bible gave birth to what is certainly the most quoted work in the English language.

He it was who found the unforgettable phrases: 'Though I speak in the tongues of men and angels but have not charity'; 'Blessed are they that mourn, they shall be comforted'; 'The last enemy to be destroyed is death. . .' Moynahan praises him for the 'sadness and rejoicing of the Eucharist': 'This is my blood of the New Testament, which shall be shed for many for the forgiveness of sins.' Add to this the 'Our Father who art in Heaven, hallowed be thy name', and we begin to glimpse our debt to him. Indeed, Tyndale wrote at the dawn of the English language and at the birth of the printing press, so that some of his translations/inventions are so deeply embedded in the language that we can't imagine it without them: 'An eye for an eye and a tooth for a tooth'; 'the spirit is willing but the flesh is weak'; 'The Lord bless thee and keep thee, the Lord make his face shine upon thee and be merciful unto thee; the Lord lift up his countenance upon thee and give thee peace.' All these come from Tyndale's brilliant translator/poet's mind.

It is hard for us today to stand in the shoes or sit in the culture of those who were discovering the Bible for themselves in their own language for the first time. It is hard for us to imagine the hatred and invective hurled against them. According to Sir Thomas More (canonised by the Roman Catholic Church in 1935), Tyndale was 'a hell-hound in the kennel of the devil . . . discharging a filthy foam of blasphemies out of his brutish mouth'. His New Testament was 'as full of errors as the sea is of water'.[2]

And yet, for those discovering the Scriptures, that same water was like drink to a dehydrated and dying body. One important influence on Tyndale and also on Latimer was Thomas Bilney. A fellow of Trinity Hall, Cambridge, the work of 'Little Bilney' among the poor made him well loved. He laboured for 'the desperates'; he was a 'preacher to the prisoners and comfortless', and particularly to lepers. His description of reading 1 Timothy shows the extraordinary impact the Bible could make on people who, in an age that knew only the seductive religiosity of the Church, now came across the word of God itself. The Bible was older than the Church, but it felt like new manna to starving souls. It had detonating effects and would eventually cost Bilney his life. 'It did so exhilarate my heart, being before wounded with the guilt of my sins, and being almost in despair.' He wrote of the discovery of St Paul and justification by faith 'that immediately I felt a marvellous comfort and quietness insomuch that my bruised bones leapt for joy'. He found that the Bible became 'more pleasant to me than the honey or the honeycomb, wherein I learnt that all my travails, all my fasting and watching, all the redemption of masses and pardons, being done without trust in Christ, who only saveth his people from their sins, these, I say, I learnt to be nothing else but even . . . a hasty running out of the right way.'[3]

Tyndale had just the same view of the life-changing power of the Scriptures. This is why he devoted his life to their translation. The process by which he came to that calling was gradual but simple, unavoidable and inevitable for one gripped by a sense of his destiny and by the gross apostasy of the Church of his day as he perceived it. The story is narrated by Foxe and others of how Tyndale became 'God's mattock to shake the inward roots and foundation of the Pope's proud prelacy'.[4]

He was educated at Magdalen College School, Oxford, from the age of twelve, studying at Magdalen and then taking his Oxford BA at Hertford College, where the best-known painting of him hangs in the dining hall. It shows a kindly, thoughtful man pointing at a Bible with the inscription, 'William Tyndale, Martyr: To scatter Roman Darkness by this Light, the loss of land and life I'll reckon slight.'

He deemed Oxford 'a place gladsome and fertile, suitable for a habitation of the gods', but found the teaching of Scripture 'so locked up with such false expositions and with false principles of natural philosophy' that students were kept outside the Bible, 'disputing all their lives about words and vain opinions pertaining as much to the healing of a man's heel as to the health of his soul'. He moved to Cambridge, where Richard Croke gave the first public lecture on the Greek language in 1518 at Cambridge. So it was that Tyndale collected the vital tools for his future trade.

Further pieces of a divine jigsaw puzzle were moved forward when Luther had nailed his 95 theses to the church door in Wittenberg in 1517, about a year after Tyndale had gone to Cambridge. The particular complaint was the sale of 'indulgences' (expensive paper forgivenesses) to pay for the lavish St Peter's Basilica in Rome. In England too there was cause for complaint. Cardinal Wolsey was the most extravagant priest ever seen in England. The university addressed him as 'Majestas' and he was plundering wherever he could to build the palace-like Cardinal's College (now Christ Church, Oxford). Tyndale revolted against this, believing as he did in the call to poverty of the priesthood. He called Wolsey 'Wolfsea . . . this wily wolf, I say, this raging sea, and shipwreck of all England . . . utterly appointed to dissemble, to have one thing in the heart and another in the mouth'.

In addition there was mass absenteeism of the clergy. The last three Bishops of Worcester, Tyndale's own diocese, were Italians who lived in Rome off their Worcester taxes. None had been seen in England. Add to this widespread ignorance with clergy who knew little of the Bible. Corruption reigned and the country groaned. The land was mourning and it seems that Tyndale, and before him Wycliffe, came to his witness/martyr calling 'for such a time as this. . .'.[5] The pieces in the battle were being called into position. Luther, while meditating on the book of Romans on the theme of justification by faith, said he 'felt as if I had been reborn altogether and had entered paradise'. It was then that 'the face of the whole of Scripture became apparent to me'.

Tyndale certainly collided with Luther's ideas at Cambridge. Perhaps he met with other later Cambridge Reformers, Latimer and Cranmer, at the White Horse pub. But it was after he moved to Gloucester that two decisive meetings took place. The first was with 'a sympathetic ancient doctor'[6] who after some conversation said, 'Do you not know that the pope is the very antichrist whom the scripture speaketh of?' He then added this: 'Beware of what you say, for if you are perceived to be of that opinion, it will cost you your life.' At the second meeting, a disputation with a 'learned man', Tyndale was confronted with the establishment view that 'we are better off without God's laws than the Pope's'. This seems to have provoked the decision, and Tyndale famously replied, 'I defy the pope and all his laws. If God spares me I will cause ere many years, the boy that drives the plough to know more of the scripture than you do!'

These words were in the end to make him a fugitive. He attempted to gain support for the translation project from the Bishop of London, which was a naïve and dangerous move. But with the help of others the brave project began.

The reasons behind the persecution came from the clear break with papal power provoked by Tyndale's project. When people began to read that Tyndale translated 'church' as 'congregation' and 'bishop' as 'elder', and saw that in the Bible there was actually no mention of purgatory, or of the mass, or of transubstantiation, or of the celibacy of the priesthood, or indeed really of the priesthood, they questioned the status quo. When it became clear that the means of peace with God was not inevitably through the Church but through Christ, a whole ancient edifice began to shift on its very foundations, threatening a catastrophic crash for the old order of things.

Tyndale said the reasons that moved him to translate the Gospels were so simple that 'he supposed it superfluous' to explain them. 'For who is so blind as to ask why light should be shown them that walk in darkness where they cannot but stumble . . . And to stumble is the danger of eternal damnation.'[7] Why did he labour on the translations with such quiet diligence? 'I answer that the love of God compelleth me. For as long as my soul feeleth what love God has showed me in Christ, I cannot but love God again and his will and commandments and out of love *work them*.' He had, he said, 'prayed, sorrowed, longed, sighed and sought' to be of God.[8]

Soon he sensed the net drawing in about him and fled to the continent. Tyndale's dynamite was eventually wrapped between the covers in 1526. To understand what he thought he was doing, we have but to look at his preface to the New Testament. He says that this is the very word of God, speaking now in English: 'If we come to these words with a pure mind, and a single eye to the words of health and eternal life, by the which if we repent and believe them we are born anew, created afresh, and enjoy the fruits of the blood of Christ. . .' In this preface he has a clear evangelical understanding – he talks of the 'fruits of the blood of Christ'; he speaks of 'That blood which cryeth, not for vengeance as the blood of Abel. Instead it has purchased life, love, favour, grace, blessing . . . It is Christ's blood that standeth between us and wrath, vengeance, curse . . . So thou shalt not despair . . . but shall feel God as a kind and merciful Father; and that his spirit shall be strong in thee, and the promises shall be given thee at the last.'

These promises and this escape from despair were not just of academic interest, since to possess a copy of this book meant arrest and possibly death. Nevertheless, the English devoured the books as they arrived in shiploads, smuggled in from Antwerp.

In the end, Sir Thomas More began to make it his prevailing passion to spy out, to root out and to burn out the men of the gospel, the evangelical sympathisers. His hatred for Tyndale was all-consuming. According to Moynahan, 'it unhinged him'. He celebrated the burning of Tyndale's fellow evangelicals with rapture. 'Tyndale's books and their own malice maketh them hereticks. And after the fire of Smithfield, hell doth receive them where they burn for ever.' More said of John Frith, 'I fear me sore that Christ will kindle a fyre of faggots for him and make him therein sweat the blood out of his body here and straight from thence his soul for ever into the fyre of hell.' More says of Tyndale and his like that they should 'have a hot iron thrust through their blasphemous tongues'.[9]

So it is that Little Bilney is taken and burned, as is Tyndale's brave friend John Frith, who had been influential in disseminating the New Testament. What was going through the minds of the martyrs/witnesses as they saw the net draw in around them, as they continued to risk death and speak out, as they refused to be silenced? We gain a vital clue to this in the letter Tyndale sent to John Frith in prison in London. In words anticipating Latimer's letter to the faithful from his prison in Oxford, Tyndale writes:

Dearly beloved, fear not men that threat, but trust Him that is true of promise. Your cause is Christ's gospel, a cause that must be fed with the blood of faith. If when we are buffeted for well doing, we suffer patiently and endure, it is thankful with God, for to that end we are called. For Christ also suffered for us, leaving an example that we may follow in His steps, who did no sin . . . Let not your body faint. If the pain be above your strength, remember: 'Whatsoever you shall ask in My name, I

will give it to you.' And pray to your father, that He will ease
your pain, or shorten it. . .[10]

In the end, Tyndale was taken through the betrayal of
one Henry Phillips. His main accusations were the self-
incriminations of his writings. He had written that he
denied the existence of purgatory, the papal supremacy, the
efficacy of prayers to saints, pilgrimage, confession to
priests. Perhaps at the root of it all was the discovery that
faith alone justifies: that safety with God and reconciliation
and peace with God flow from the forgiveness of sins
offered through belief in the sacrifice of Christ – the good
news of the gospel. Each of these was enough for him to be
burnt as a heretic. And now, he made his own defence, not
trying to avoid the consequences of his position. Here he
was true to his fearless character which clung to the rock of
the truth. Years earlier, he had not altered his convictions
even to accommodate Henry VIII in his quest to be divorced.
Had he done so, his story would no doubt have been different. At his trial, nothing shifted.

And so it was that the day eventually dawned for him to
be taken to the gallows and the fire: twin punishments for
treason (the gallows) and for heresy (the fire).

We will turn to *Foxe's Book of Martyrs* for the last word on
Tyndale, remarking that the world still waits for the courageous imitators of this godly champion of the truth to take
their place in the courts of the New Europe.

Master Tyndale had so preached to them who had him in
charge, and such as was there conversant with him in the
Castle that they reported of him, that if he were not a good
Christian man, they knew not whom they might take to be one.

At last, after much reasoning, when no reason would serve, although he deserved no death, he was condemned by virtue of the emperor's decree, made in the assembly at Augsburg. Brought forth to the place of execution, he was tied to the stake, strangled by the hangman, and afterwards consumed with fire, at the town of Vilvoorde, AD 1536; crying at the stake with a fervent zeal, and a loud voice, 'Lord! open the king of England's eyes.'

Such was the power of his doctrine, and the sincerity of his life, that during the time of his imprisonment (which endured a year and a half), he converted, it is said, his keeper, the keeper's daughter, and others of his household.

As touching his translation of the New Testament, because his enemies did so much carp at it, pretending it to be full of heresies, he wrote to John Frith, as followeth, 'I call God to record against the day we shall appear before our Lord Jesus, that I never altered one syllable of God's Word against my conscience, nor would do this day, if all that is in earth, whether it be honour, pleasure, or riches, might be given me.'[11]

# 6

# *Latimer and Ridley*

*'Torture (at the stake) . . . was a policy of terror to make everyone aware through the body of the criminal, of the unrestrained presence of the sovereign. The theatre of terror, its ruthlessness, its spectacle, its physical violence, its meticulous ceremonial, its entire apparatus: the public execution did not re-establish justice, it re-activated power.' Michel Foucauld[1]*

The Oxford martyrs to whom we now turn call out to us still today. They held the highest office in the land. They were tried and examined in the greatest university in the continent of Europe. They wrote work which transformed the English language no less importantly than Shakespeare. One of their number, Hugh Latimer, was able to communicate with the ordinary Englishman and with the royal court in the same burning sermons. And yet they were willing to be stripped of office, lands and benefits and face the flames – all for the sake of Christ. They are an example and a warning to those seeking a destiny in God today.

England groaned and struggled through the reigns of four Tudor monarchs to shake off the heavy weight of religion and tradition which had choked the hopeful news of Christianity for so many superstitious years. Henry VIII brought an (albeit self-interested) uprooting from the influence of Rome. He elevated Thomas Cranmer to Archbishop and *The Book of Common Prayer* with its timeless, comfortable words began to be published. Under Edward VI, Henry's son, the country pushed further towards the unfettered message of Christ. Hugh Latimer preached his convicting manifesto 'On the Plough' before the young king, crying out, 'O London, Repent, repent. . .' and the Bible was unchained and its message available at last. King Edward died young, however, and then Henry's Catholic daughter Mary was crowned. The tide swung back and the waters of persecution of Protestants began to rise, before breaking mercilessly over those who would not swear allegiance to the Pope and to the mass. The greatest and bravest of English Protestants were swept into the fires to be burnt up like their apostolic predecessors. Eventually, Henry's second daughter Elizabeth, a Protestant, continued the transition of a nation where, 200 years after Wycliffe's death, Protestantism became rooted in the fabric of the land.

## Hugh Latimer[2]

Born the son of a poor farmer in Leicester, Hugh Latimer went up to Cambridge and received his bachelor's degree around 1510 and his master's degree in 1514 before beginning to study divinity. While at Cambridge, Latimer was an ardent defender of the Roman Church. In his free time, he followed the defenders of the Reformation into their meeting houses, disputed with them and implored them to abandon their convictions. He orally defended his divinity degree in 1524 by attacking the theology of the Reformer Philip Melanchthon. 'At last,' said his hearers, 'England will furnish a champion for the Church that will confront the Wittenberg doctors.'

Through the workings of Thomas Bilney, one of those with whom he had argued in the meeting houses, Latimer would undergo an immense paradigm shift. Bilney went to the college where Latimer lived, begging to make confession. Latimer thought, 'My paper against Melanchthon has no doubt converted him.' There, kneeling before Latimer, Bilney shared with him 'the anguish he had once felt in his soul', 'the efforts he had made to remove it', and 'lastly, the peace he had felt when he believed that Jesus Christ is the Lamb of God that taketh away the sins of the world'. Latimer no doubt knew this anguish – for example, each time he mixed water with wine, as the missal directed, his conscience was troubled that he did not mix enough water. Trying to live by the law and superstitions had left Latimer, like Luther before him, feeling insufficient. And so Latimer listened, trying to chase away his thoughts. But Bilney continued. When Bilney finally arose from his knees, Latimer remained seated, weeping. The gracious Bilney consoled him, 'Though your sins be as scarlet, they shall be as white as snow.'

Latimer got up from this encounter a new man. Like Paul, his zeal did not leave him – he simply switched allegiance. He was licensed to preach throughout England and it is instructive to know what he actually said. As we look at his preaching content and style, let this push us to braver, denser, more Christ-like proclamation in our land.

Latimer's sermon 'On the Plough', one of a series preached

as Bishop of Worcester before King Edward, is one bulging at the seams with pithy social comment and striking images as he moves breathtakingly from one fervently given exhortation to another. It seems to tumble from his lips. He never wavers from his central points, first the urgent need for preachers, and second the sound doctrine of Christ's death as 'the thing whereby we have salvation'. Against this he contrasts the present state and idleness of unpreaching prelates and the present uncharitable, condemnable state of London, and the activity of the devil ('the diligentest bishop in all England') against whom his hearers need to fight for their lives.

His preaching is woven inextricably into the fabric of life in England in 1548. His theological preoccupations reflect the concerns of the day, namely to expound the efficacy of Christ's sacrificial death and to attack the papist plot to 'evacuate the cross of Christ'.

Where the devil is resident and hath his plough going, there away with books, and up with candles; away with bibles and up with beads; away with the light of the gospel, and up with the light of candles, yea at noon-day. Where the devil is resident, that he may prevail, up with all superstition and idolatry; censing, painting of images, candles, palms, ashes, holy water and new service of men's inventing; as though man could invent a better way to honour God with than God himself hath appointed. Down with Christ's cross, up with purgatory pick-purse . . . Away with clothing the naked, the poor and impot-ent; up with man's traditions and his laws, down with God's traditions and his most holy word. Down with the old honour due to God and up with the new god's honour. Let all things be done in Latin. . .

This preoccupation leads Latimer into some sparkling contrasts, not only riveting for his audience to listen to and highly entertaining, but also bursting with all the passion and feeling of a man who, in his time in the Tower for such opinions, has, in the words of St Francis, 'grown hot within before speaking out words which themselves are cold'.

Latimer clearly, by the reign of Edward VI, had no more time for Roman rites and was not one to water down or 'blanch' his criticism. His reference to the 'purgatory pick-purse' is often repeated in his sermons, as are his attacks on images and the veneration of relics.

> But the devil, by help of that Italian bishop yonder, his chaplain, hath laboured by all means that he might to frustrate the death of Christ and the merits of his passion. And they have devised for that purpose to make us believe in other vain things by his pardons; as to have remission of sins for praying on hallowed beads . . . Holy water, to hallowed bells, palms, candles, ashes, and what not? And of these things, every one hath taken away some part of Christ's sanctification; every one hath robbed some part of Christ's passion and cross, and hath mingled Christ's death and hath been made to be propitiatory and satisfactory and to put away sin.

Here he shows his scorn by means of a description of the mechanics of superstition. However, Latimer is very clear why he objects to these things and it is always for the same reason, namely that he wishes to give a proper account of the propitiatory death of Christ. The following passage shows his awareness in his day of the need to give a proper explanation to this long-lost teaching.

Now if I should preach in the country, among the unlearned, I would tell what propitiatory, expiatory, and remissory is; but here is a learned auditory: yet for them that be unlearned I will expound it. Propitiatory, expiatory, remissory, or satisfactory, for they signify all one thing in effect and is nothing else but a thing whereby to obtain remission of sins and to have salvation. And this way the devil used to evacuate the death of Christ, that we might have affiance in other things, as in the sacrifice of the priest; whereas Christ would have us to trust in his only sacrifice. So he was, *'Agnus occisus ab origine mundi'*; 'The Lamb that hath been slain from the beginning of the world'; and therefore he is called *'juge sacrificium'*, 'a continual sacrifice'; and not for the continuance of the mass, as the blanchers have blanched it, and wrested it; and as I myself did once betake it. But Paul saith, *'per semetipsum purgation facta'*; 'By himself,' and by none other, Christ 'made purgation' and satisfaction for the whole world.

Would Christ this word, 'by himself', had been better weighed and looked upon, and *'in sanctificationem'*, to make them holy; for he is *'juge sacrificium'*, 'a continual sacrifice', in effect, fruit and operation; that like as they, which seeing the serpent hang up in the desert, were put in remembrance of Christ's death, in whom as many as believed were saved; so all men that trusted in the death of Christ shall be saved, as well they that were before, as they that came after. For he was a continual sacrifice, as I said, in effect, fruit, operation, and virtue; as though he had from the beginning of the world, and continually should to the world's end, hang still on the cross; and he is as fresh hanging on the cross now, to them that believe and trust in him, as he was fifteen hundred years ago, when he was crucified.

Then let us trust upon his death, and look for none other sacrifice propitiatory.

'Thus began', writes Merle d'Aubigne, 'in British Christendom the preaching of the cross. The Reformation was not the substitution of the catholicism of the first ages for the popery of the Middle Ages. It was a revival of the preaching of St Paul and thus it was that on hearing Latimer (after his conversion), everyone exclaimed with rapture: "Of a Saul God has made him a very Paul".'[3] It is noteworthy that Latimer's preaching of the cross is concise and clear and constantly enhanced by the contrast between it and any other 'sacrifice propitiatory'. He habitually quotes the Scriptures in Latin first and then follows with an English translation, as here. He had preached in Cambridge on the need for the Bible to be read in the vulgar tongue as soon as he heard of Tyndale's new translation. But he continued to quote first in Latin, probably out of a desire to show his texts as being authentic and authoritative. Of the authority of Scripture he had no doubts:

> The Author of Holy Scripture is the Mighty One, the Everlasting, God Himself and this Scripture partakes of the Might and Eternity of its Author. There is neither king nor emperor that is not bound to obey it. Let us beware of those by-paths of human tradition, filled with stones, brambles and uprooted trees. Let us follow the straight road of the Word. It does not concern us what the fathers have done, but what they should have done.

His application of biblical truth is always particularly earthed in the abuses of his own day and we learn of these with some precision. Latimer tells us of burgesses who are greedy, envious, cruel and merciless; of London paupers lying sick in the streets and dying of hunger; of the ending of poor relief and the maintenance of poor scholars. He tells us much about the clergy of his day:

> For ever since the prelates were made lords and nobles, the plough standeth; there is no work done, the people starve. They hawk, they hunt, they card, they dice; they pastime in their prelacies with gallant gentlemen, with their dancing minions and with their fresh companions, so that ploughing is set aside: and by their lording and loitering, preaching and ploughing is clean gone.

This picture gives an illuminating idea of the scandal of his day. Similarly his description of the clergy's preoccupation with other lucrative employment:

> They are otherwise occupied, some in the king's matters, some are ambassadors, some of the privy council, some to furnish the court, some are lords of the parliament, some are presidents and comptrollers of mints.

This application of his message of the plough is, as it should be, precisely grounded in contemporary society. Latimer shows his awareness of the need to pray for the government of the country, as the king comes under pressure from 'blanchers' who would halt the progress of the Reformation.

Latimer's skill in making his message inseparable from the context into which he preaches it is found in his exploitation of the image of 'preacher as ploughman'.[4]

> A prelate is that man, whatsoever he be, that hath a flock to be taught of him; whosoever hath any spiritual charge in the faithful congregation and whosoever he be that hath cure of souls. And well may the preacher and the ploughman be

likened together: first, for their labour of all seasons of the year; for there is no time of the year in which the ploughman hath not some special work to do: as in my county in Leicestershire, the ploughman hath a time to set forth, and to assay his plough and other times for other necessary works to be done. And then they also may be likened together for the diversity of works and variety of offices that they have to do. For as the ploughman first setteth forth his plough, and then tilleth his land, and breaketh it in furrows, and sometime ridgeth it up again: and at another time harroweth and clotteth it, and sometime dungeth it and hedgeth it, diggeth it and weedeth it, purgeth and maketh it clean: so the prelate, the preacher, hath many diverse offices to do.

He hath first a busy work to bring his parishioners to a right faith, as Paul calleth it, and not a swerving faith; but to a faith that embraceth Christ, and trusteth to his merits; a lively faith, a justifying faith; a faith that maketh a man righteous, without respect of works: as ye have it very well declared and set forth in the Homily. He hath then a busy work, I say, to bring his flock to a right faith, and then to confirm them in the same faith: now casting them down with the law, and with the threatenings of God for sin; now ridging them up again with the gospel, and with the promises of God's favour: now weeding them, by telling them their faults, and making them forsake sin; now clotting them, by breaking their stony hearts and by making them supplehearted and making them to have hearts of flesh; that is, soft hearts, and apt for doctrine to enter in: now teaching to know God rightly and to know their duty to God and their neighbours: now exhorting them, when they know their duty, that they do it, and be diligent in it; so that they have a continual work to do.

## Words on fire

Latimer shows a natural wit and skill in holding his audience. Notable are his frequent alliterations, here coupled with biting criticism of the clergy.

> But now for the fault of unpreaching prelates, methink I could guess what might be said for excusing of them. They are so troubled with lordly living, they be so placed in palaces, couched in courts, ruffling in their rents, dancing in their dominions, burdened with ambassages, pampering of their paunches, like a monk that maketh his jubilee; munching in their mangers, and moiling in their gay manors and mansions and so troubled with loitering in their lordships, that they cannot attend it.

Such verbal facility, coupled with a common honesty and righteousness evident in Latimer, must have delighted his listeners. Latimer is fond too of sharp contrasts and seems to have seen things in a particularly black-and-white way.

> Since lording and loitering hath come up, preaching hath come down . . . Down with Christ's cross . . . up with purgatory pickpurse . . . Away with clothing the naked . . . up with decking of images . . . Down with God's traditions and most holy word . . . up with man's tradition and his laws . . . Down with the old honour due to God . . . up with the new god's honour. . .

These contrasts push an audience towards a clear choice and as such all add to the persuasiveness of Latimer's message. One of his greatest abilities was to find a telling image to hold his audience's attention and to make his point. This at times is done to comic effect, as in this reference:

For the preaching of the word of God unto the people is called meat: scripture calleth it meat; not strawberries, that come but once a year, and tarry not long, but are soon gone: but it is meat, it is not dainties. The people must have meat that must be familiar and continual, and daily given unto them to feed upon. Many make a strawberry of it, ministering it but once a year; but such do not the office of good prelates.

The whole sermon is based, of course, on an illustration that Jesus gave: that of the preacher as ploughman. One of the most famous examples of Latimer's preaching has to do with his illustration of the devil as preacher:

And now I would ask a strange question: who is the most diligentest bishop and prelate in all England, that passeth all the rest in doing his office? I can tell, for I know him who it is; I know him well. But now I think I see you listening and hearkening that I should name him. There is one that passeth all the other and is the most diligent prelate and preacher in all England. And will ye know who it is? I will tell you: it is the Devil. He is the most diligent preacher of all other; he is never out of his diocese; he is never from his cure; ye shall never find him unoccupied; he is ever in his parish; he keepeth residence at all times; ye shall never find him out of the way, call for him when you will he is ever at home; the diligentest preacher in all the realm; he is ever at his plough: no lording nor loitering can hinder him; he is ever applying his business, ye shall never find him idle, I warrant you. And his office is to hinder religion, to maintain superstition, to set up idolatry, to teach all kind of popery . . . But here some man will say to me, 'What, sir, are ye so privy of the Devil's counsel, that ye know all this to be true?' Truly I know him too well, and have obeyed him a little too much in condescending to some follies; and I know him as other men do, yea, that he is ever occupied, and ever busy in following his plough. I know by St Peter, which saith of him, *'Sicut leo rugiens circuit quoerens quem devoret'*: 'He goeth about like a roaring lion, seeking whom he may devour.'

The power of this passage comes not so much from the idea of the devil as preacher, but from the manner in which Latimer exploits the illustration. First, he builds up suspense as to who this diligent preacher is – Latimer's ability to introduce suspense is constantly evident in his preaching. Second, he takes enjoyment in piling detail upon detail of this never-loitering, ever-ploughing prelate, finally bringing in the authority of the Scriptures to add weight again to his point. Latimer was so aware of the need to put flesh and blood onto the ideas he sought to express that he frequently introduced personal testimony. Here he admits, 'I know [the devil] too well, and have obeyed him a little too much in condescending to some follies,' probably referring to his former adherence to Roman doctrines.

Latimer was a preacher who combined the faith in Christ of the Reformation with a longing to see it lived out in the everyday lives of his congregations. In a day of no worldwide web, where the invention of the printing press was only comparatively recent, we should remember the immense influence of the pulpit and note that Latimer was a popular preacher in the true sense of the term. From the days of his conversion, when he had heard the confession of Thomas Bilney in Cambridge as to the way to peace with God through the atoning death of Christ, he began to turn his zeal for asceticism for which he was noted into an evangelical zeal to bring good news to the poor. So it was that he and Bilney visited the madhouse and the leper colony and found the gates of Cambridge jail open to them as they fed the hungry, visited the sick and those in prison and tried to comfort all with the gospel. This work continued for some years with some fruitfulness, as Latimer mentions in his fifth sermon years later to Edward VI:

> One woman prisoner was all on her beads, and savoured not of Jesus Christ. In process, she tasted that the Lord is gracious. She had such a savour, such a sweetness and feeling that she thought it long to the day of execution. She was with Christ already, as touching faith, longing to depart and be with Him.

This steadfast faith became Latimer's own. Two long letters written from his last imprisonment show how completely reliant he became on the word of God as he found it in the New Testament:

> The wise men of the world can find shifts to avoid the cross; but the simple servant of Christ does look for no other, but oppression in the world . . . For as long as we are in the body, we are strangers to God and far from our native country, which is heaven, where our everlasting day is. We are now more near to God than ever we were . . . We have found the precious stone of the gospel; for the which we ought to sell all that we have in the world . . . The martyrs of old times were racked . . . and would not be delivered, that they might have a better resurrection.
>
> Let us follow them, and leave the pope's market, who buyeth and selleth the bodies and souls of men . . . Embrace Christ's cross, and Christ shall embrace you.

For his biographer, Darby, this is a letter in which Latimer addresses himself and gives himself courage. But that courage remained till the end. In his second letter, intended to be read by many in the coming persecution, he recalls the enormous number of kings, patriarchs, prophets, apostles, evangelists, children of God and saints who found the warnings of their Lord literally fulfilled in martyrdom, and then says:

> But if none of these were, if you had no other company to go with you, yet have you me, your poorest brother and bondsman in the Lord, with many other I trust in God. But if you had none of these . . . yet you have your general captain and master: Christ Jesus, the dear darling and only beloved Son of God, in whom was all the Father's joy and delectation. You have him to go before you: no fairer was his way than ours, but much worse and fouler, towards the city of the heavenly Jerusalem. . .

With these and other words of faith and love for Christ, he strengthened his brethren and himself.

Having understood the gospel, having attacked its opponents, having sought to apply gospel truth to ordinary lives, Latimer in the end had to suffer death through burning. Latimer followed Paul, Polycarp, Tyndale and his brother Bilney. Long before Richard Baxter's time, Latimer anticipated his saying and preached 'as a dying man to dying men'.

## Latimer's courage

With Thomas Bilney, Latimer had found peace with God. Like Wesley, his heart was strangely warmed by trusting in Christ alone. This became the cause for which he was ultimately prepared to suffer imprisonment and death if need be. Yet what is impressive is that it was not a flaky 'enthusiasm', but a proclamation of the highest intelligence made before the authorities of the land. How we need this today. In a sermon before Henry VIII, he began by speaking out loud, exclaiming, 'Latimer, Latimer, thou art going to speak before the high and mighty king, Henry VIII, who is able, if he think fit, to take thy life away. Be careful what thou sayest. But Latimer, Latimer, remember thou art also about to speak before the King of kings and Lord of lords. Take heed thou dost not displease Him.'

He was appointed Bishop of Worcester under Henry VIII. But Henry swung unpredictably from old Catholicism to biblical Christianity and back again. Latimer felt he was left with no choice but to resign in 1539 when he was forced to comply with the Six Articles, a return to Roman doctrines he opposed. As he threw off the robes of his bishopric, he leaped into the air, and declared that he found himself lighter than he had ever felt before. How this remains a challenge to bishops and all those in high office today. He was later put into prison for a short period of time, but was released in 1547 with the accession of Edward VI. He spent the next six years of his life as a humble preacher, residing with his dear friend Thomas Cranmer.

On the accession of Mary, the tide turned again and Latimer was speedily arrested and imprisoned, first in the Tower of London and then in the Bocardo. Pulled down in 1771, this was the common jail in Oxford, next to St Michael's in the North Gate.

On the 30th September 1554, the trials of Latimer and Ridley began in the divinity schools of Oxford. They swiftly ended in condemnation of both as heretics. They were degraded from their office of priest as Tyndale had been before them.

## Nicholas Ridley

In 1534 Nicholas Ridley, while a proctor of Cambridge, signed the decree against the Pope's supremacy in England. In 1537 he became chaplain to Thomas Cranmer, in 1540 master of Pembroke Hall, Cambridge, and in 1541 chaplain to Henry VIII. Under the reign of Edward he became Bishop of Rochester (1547) and was part of the committee that drew up the first English *Book of Common Prayer*. As Bishop of Rochester, Ridley was chosen to strengthen and establish the Reformed teachings at Cambridge. In 1550 he became Bishop of London, where he did much to improve the condition of the poor by preaching on social injustices before the king. In 1553, shortly after the accession of Mary, he was imprisoned.

On the evening before his execution, 'good master Ridley' was entertained to an excellent supper at Mr and Mrs Irish's home, where he had been under house arrest. Ridley was in the best of spirits and 'very facetious', saying, like so many Protestants, that he regarded his martyrdom next day as his marriage. He said that he hoped they would all attend his 'marriage feast' and the Catholic Mrs Irish, who had been won over by the example of Ridley, was 'very moved and sad that Ridley was to die'.[5] Ridley remarked to her, 'Though my breakfast will be somewhat sharp, my supper will be more pleasant and sweet.'

On the 16th October 1555, Ridley and Latimer were led to their martyrdom. Ridley came fully robed, as he would be dressed as a bishop. Latimer wore a simple frieze frock. Ridley had had a good night's sleep and walked happily to the stake. Seeing Latimer behind him, he called out, 'O be ye there?' The 70-year-old Latimer followed feebly behind and replied, 'Yea as fast as I can follow.' Ridley gave his clothes away to those standing by. Latimer quietly stripped to his shroud. Though in his clothes he appeared a withered, crooked old man, he now stood bolt upright. As they were fastened to their stakes, Ridley's brother tied a bag of gunpowder to both of their necks. And then, as a burning faggot was laid at the feet of Ridley, Latimer spoke his famous words, 'Be of good cheer, Master Ridley, and play the man; we shall this day light such a candle, by God's grace, in England, as I trust shall never be put out.'

John Foxe relates the rest:

And so the fire being kindled, when Ridley saw the fire flaming up towards him, he cried with a loud voice, 'Lord into Thy hands I commend my spirit: Lord, receive my spirit!' and repeated the latter part often. Latimer, crying as vehemently on the other side of the stake, 'Father of heaven, receive my soul!' received the flame as if embracing it. After he had stroked his face with his hands, and as it were bathed them a little in the fire, he soon died, as it appeared, with very little pain.[6]

Latimer, who lived and died unmarried, eased out of this world. But it was not so with his friend Nicholas Ridley. The faggots being piled too high, he screamed for his bystanders to pull off some of the wood. Misunderstanding him, his brother-in-law added more sticks to the fire. The fire 'burned clean all his nether parts, before it once touched the upper; and that made him often desire them to let the fire come unto him'. He exclaimed, 'I cannot burn!' When he turned to his watchers, they saw a ghastly sight. 'After his legs were consumed he showed that side towards us clean, shirt and all untouched with flame.' Finally, a bystander pulled the faggots from the fire, and the fire flamed to his face, igniting the gunpowder. He stirred no more. And as hundreds of bystanders looked on at these two motionless bodies, all that could be heard was weeping.

# 7

## *Archbishop Thomas Cranmer*

*'For it now pleases God to accomplish that which I have many times desired, as you well know: namely that he grant me the grace to die for his gospel, to the edification of his people. This he will do in the near future, delivering me from all evils and setting me in his kingdom.' Pierre Brully*[1]

Thomas Cranmer went to Cambridge at the age of 14 in 1503, and turned to the new biblical theology and the study of the sacred languages. He became a fellow of Jesus College but resigned when, as Morice puts it, 'He chanced to marry a wife.'[2] Suddenly, because of his immense, careful talent, in 1529 this 'remote and ineffectual don' was snatched into the world of affairs in the interests of the king's great cause, the royal divorce. He defended the position that Henry's marriage to Catherine of Aragon was null and void, collecting opinions in his favour from the universities. Cranmer went to Rome to argue the king's case and was an ambassador to the Holy Roman Emperor Charles V. In 1533 Henry named him Archbishop of Canterbury, and as soon as the appointment was confirmed by the Pope, Cranmer proclaimed that Henry's marriage to Catherine was invalid.

Henry perhaps chose Cranmer in order not to have to fight with another strong, dominating or 'turbulent' priest.[3] For Cranmer was not a leader in the sense of a party leader and in a crisis was wont to make his protest quietly and firmly and then retire to his study or his diocese. But intercede he did, with a king whose rage was easily ignited. He defended in turn More[4] and Fisher, Ann Boleyn and Thomas Cromwell as each fell from favour. Cranmer believed in the doctrine of the 'godly prince' to whom Christians are called to submit. At the end of Henry's life, it was Cranmer who was with him on his deathbed.

> Then the archbishop, exhorting him to put his trust in Christ, and to call upon his mercy, desired him, though he could not speak, yet to give some token with his eyes or with his hand, that he trusted in the Lord. Then the king, holding him with his hand, did wring his hand in his as hard as he could. . .[5]

Thus his biographer Diarmaid MacCulloch concludes:

> Quietly playing out his calling as royal chaplain, Cranmer had won a final victory in his years of argument with the king on justification. No last rites for Henry; no extreme unction: just an evangelical statement of faith in a grip of a hand. Thus ended the longest relationship of love that either man had known.[6]

Cranmer was strongly influenced by the German Reformation. He endorsed the translation of the Bible into English and was influential in procuring a royal proclamation in 1538 providing for a copy in every parish church. However, as long as Henry VIII lived, the Archbishop could promote no significant doctrinal changes. The situation changed with the accession in 1547 of the young Edward VI, during whose reign Cranmer shaped the doctrinal and liturgical transformation of the Church of England. He was responsible for much of the first *Book of Common Prayer* (1549) and compiled the revision of 1552. This matchless document contains in essence what Cranmer preached. For example, some of the homilies in *The Book of Common Prayer* express his careful, balanced thought, at once Augustinian and evangelical. Behind all his words there is deep scholarship and fine patristic wisdom. His private collection of books is said to have outnumbered the university library. He pleaded the evangelical cause as among the wisest and most articulate in the land. We can turn to his matchless prose to see his hopeful theology:

> We do not presume to come to this thy table, O merciful Lord, trusting in our own righteousness, but in thy manifold and great mercies. . .

Or again:

> Almighty God, unto whom all hearts be open, all desires known, and from whom no secrets are hid: cleanse the thoughts of our hearts by the inspiration of thy Holy Spirit, that we may perfectly love thee, and worthily magnify thy holy name. . .

He believed that it was necessary to transform the mass into a 'communion of the faithful', and that the abuses contained in the sacrifice of the mass required a surgical, major operation on the previous form of service. In this he cannot be clearer about the central tenet of this newly discovered evangelical faith: the once-for-all-ness of the cross.

Who made there, by his one oblation of himself once offered, a full, perfect, and sufficient sacrifice, oblation, and satisfaction for the sins of the whole world.

There is nothing quite as emphatic as this in any other Protestant liturgy of the Reformation. If Latimer was the beginning of the preaching of the cross, Cranmer was the architect of the liturgy of the cross. As such, his evangelical words were to be memorised by 20 generations of Anglicans and beyond.

After Edward's death, when Mary came to the throne, Cranmer was in a quandary. He had believed that it is the duty of every Christian to obey the monarch, and that 'the powers that be are ordained of God' (Rom. 13:1 KJV). As long as the monarch was ordering things that Cranmer thought good, it was easy for Cranmer to believe that the king was sent by God's providence to guide the people in the path of true religion, and that disobedience to the king was disobedience to God. Now Mary was queen and commanding him to return to the Roman obedience. Five times Cranmer wrote a letter of submission to the Pope and to Roman Catholic doctrines, and four times he tore it up. In the end, he submitted. However, Mary was unwilling to believe that the submission was sincere, and he was imprisoned in the Tower, some 22 years after he had become Archbishop.

Ordered to Oxford along with Latimer and Ridley for a formal university disputation on the Eucharist in 1555, he stood firm to his evangelical views despite being harassed and ridiculed, interrupted and harangued in an unusual display of university venom. Cranmer's thinking on this had been variously influenced in the past by, among others, Bucer, who wrote to him, 'We acknowledge that the bread and wine do not change on nature, but they become signs . . . by which signs (Christ) indeed may be offered to everyone.'[7] This position had strengthened when Peter Martyr had brought him a lost manuscript of an epistle by John Chrysostom containing a passage which included 'a perfect patristic basis for bread that remained a sign', including as it did the phrase 'the nature of the bread doth still remain' after consecration.[8]

We may today find it hard to get excited about these issues which seem marginal. Each age has its own disputes. Ours are more likely to have to do with speaking out on ethical and lifestyle issues, and daring to stand for the uniqueness of Christ in the face of new laws on 'religious hatred'. But at the time the power of the Roman Church, enshrined in non-biblical additions which only the Roman Church could dispense, was being challenged by Cranmer in this vital issue. He was calling out for the simplicity of access to Christ, and the powers of the age, wanting to retain their monopoly, were about to kill him for it.

The dispute was disorganised, moving from Latin to English and back again. Cranmer's arguments were as dense and strong as befitted one who had made the subject the study of a lifetime. When at the end he was inevitably condemned with the others to have been overcome in argument, he burst out, 'How could he argue when four or five interrupted him at a time?' In the end, quoting one of his own articles of religion, the ex-archbishop concluded,

'From this your judgement and sentence, I appeal to the just judgement of God almighty, trusting to be present with him in heaven, for whose presence in the altar I am thus condemned.'[9]

Cranmer was taken to prison where, having witnessed the agony of Ridley's death, he was persuaded to renounce his Reformed faith. Like Galileo before the Inquisition, when they showed him the instruments of torture, he crumbled. Cranmer in the end signed no fewer than six recantations, each more grovelling than the last, all of which were ceremoniously published and which his supporters immediately accused of being falsified. But they were not. Cranmer had succumbed to fear; succumbed to his desire for life; slipping in perhaps his desire to obey his monarch as his only excuse. This is some of the first of the recantations:

> I, Thomas Cranmer, late archbishop of Canterbury, do renounce, abhor, and detest all manner of heresies and errors of Luther and Zwingli . . . And I believe most constantly in my heart, and with my mouth I confess one holy and Catholic Church visible, without which there is no salvation; and therefore I acknowledge the Bishop of Rome to be supreme head on earth, whom I acknowledge to be the highest bishop and pope, and Christ's vicar, unto whom all Christian people ought to be subject. And as concerning the sacraments, I believe and worship in the sacrament of the altar the body and blood of Christ, being contained most truly under the forms of bread and wine; the bread, through the mighty power of God being turned into the body of our Saviour Jesus Christ, and the wine into His blood . . . Furthermore, I believe that there is a place of purgatory, where souls departed be punished for a time, for whom the Church doth godily and wholesomely pray, like as it doth

honour saints and make prayers to them. Finally . . . I am sorry
that I ever held or thought otherwise. And I beseech Almighty
God, that of His mercy He will vouchsafe to forgive me whatsoever I have offended against God or His Church . . . And to
conclude, as I submit myself to the Catholic Church of Christ,
and to the supreme head thereof, so I submit myself unto the
most excellent majesties of Philip and Mary, king and queen of
this realm of England, etc. And God is my witness, that I have
not done this for favour or fear of any person, but willingly and
of mine own conscience, as to the instruction of others.

And yet soon the news came that despite this repentance, he
was still to be burnt as punishment and as an example. This
is what has been called 'The Great Miscalculation'.[10] Somehow this turned Cranmer back to his true opinions. Nothing in his behaviour the day before his martyrdom showed
he was about to turn from betrayal to brilliant bravery. For
the telling of this story we will weave Foxe's account with
our own précis of events. Foxe takes up the story:

> In this so great expectation (on 25 March 1556) Cranmer at
> length comes from the Bocardo into St Mary's Church (the
> University Church). Because it was a foul and rainy day, in this
> order: the mayor went before; next him the aldermen in their
> place and degree; after them was Cranmer between two friars
> which, mumbling to-and-fro certain Psalms in the streets,
> answered one another until they came to the church door and
> there they began the Song of Simeon, Nunc Dimittis, and en-
> tering into the church the Psalm-singing friars brought him to
> his landing place and left him there. There was a stage set over
> against the pulpit, of a mean height from the ground, where
> Cranmer had his standing, waiting until Cole made him ready
> to his sermon.

The lamentable case and sight of that man gave a sorrowful spectacle to all Christian eyes that beheld him. He that late was Archbishop, Metropolitan, and Primate of all England and the King's Privy Councillor, being now in a bare and ragged gown and ill favouredly clothed, exposed to the contempt of all men, did admonish men not only of his own calamity but also of their state and fortune . . . In this habit, when he had stood a good space on the stage, he lifted up his hands to heaven and prayed to God.

The church was crowded with people of both sides: the Catholics rejoicing, the Protestants wounded in spirit at the deceit of the human heart. Dr Cole, in his sermon, represented Cranmer as having been guilty of the most terrible crimes, and encouraged the deluded sufferer not to fear death, not to doubt the support of God in his torments, nor that masses would be said in all the churches of Oxford for the repose of his soul.

Cranmer in all this time with what grief he stood hearing the sermon, the outward shews of his Body and countenance did better express than any man can declare, one while lifting up his eyes to heaven and then again for shame letting them down to earth . . . More than twenty several times the tears gushed out abundantly dropping down marvellously from his Fatherly Face. They which were present testify they never saw in any child more tears.

When called to speak, he began by praying:

To Thee, therefore, O Lord, do I run; to Thee do I humble myself, saying, O Lord, my God, my sins be great, but yet have mercy upon me for Thy great mercy. The great mystery that God became man, was not wrought for little or few offences.

> Thou didst not give Thy Son, O Heavenly Father, unto death for small sins only, but for all the greatest sins of the world, so that the sinner return to Thee with his whole heart, as I do at present. Wherefore, have mercy on me, O God, whose property is always to have mercy, have mercy upon me, O Lord, for Thy great mercy.

Rising, he quoted three verses of the fifth chapter of James, showing that even on this most dramatic day, care for the poor was inseparable for him from believing the gospel.

> Let them that be rich ponder well these three sentences: for if they ever had occasion to show their charity, they have it now at this present, the poor people being so many, and victual so dear.

Cole then demanded that Cranmer repeat the terms of his recantation, 'that all men may understand that you are a Catholic indeed'. But Cranmer stunned the congregation by recanting his recantation.[11]

> And now forasmuch as I am come to the last end of my life, whereupon hangeth all my life past, and all my life to come, either to live with my master Christ for ever in joy, or else to be in pain for ever with the wicked in hell. . .
>
> Now I come to the great thing which so much troubleth my conscience, more than any thing that ever I did or said in my whole life, and that is the setting abroad of a writing contrary to the truth, which now here I renounce and refuse, as things written with my hand contrary to the truth which I thought in my heart, and written for fear of death, and to save my life, if it might be; and that is, all such bills or papers which I have written or signed with my hand since my degradation, wherein

I have written many things untrue. And forasmuch as my hand hath offended, writing contrary to my heart, therefore my hand shall first be punished; for when I come to the fire it shall first be burned.

Commotion – both joy and rage – was breaking out in the church, yet Cranmer kept shouting: he needed still to get two vital, last messages across. He raised his voice: 'And as for the Pope, I refuse him as Christ's enemy, and Antichrist, with all his false doctrine.' Upon the conclusion of this unexpected declaration, amazement and indignation were in every part of the church. The Catholics were completely foiled, their object being frustrated and Cranmer, like Samson, having completed a greater ruin on his enemies in the hour of death than he did in his life. 'And as for the sacrament, I believe as I have taught in my book against the Bishop of Winchester.'[12] Cranmer would have proceeded in the exposure of the doctrines he held so false, but a near riot drowned his voice and the preacher gave an order to 'lead the heretic away!'.

The savage command was directly obeyed, and the lamb about to suffer was torn from his stand to the place of slaughter, insulted all the way by the revilings and taunts of the pestilent monks and friars.

With thoughts intent upon a far higher object than the empty threats of man, he reached the spot dyed with the blood of Ridley and Latimer. A chain was provided to bind him to the stake, and after it had tightly encircled him, fire was put to the fuel, and the flames began soon to ascend. In the flames, Cranmer achieved a final serenity: he fulfilled the promise he had made at his defence, crying: 'forasmuch my hand offended, writing contrary to my heart, my hand shall first be punished'.

And when the fire began to burn near him, stretching out his arm, he put his right hand into the flame, which he held so steadfast and immovable (saving that once with the same hand he wiped his face) that all men might see his hand burned before his body was touched. His eyes were lifted up to heaven and often he repeated: 'This unworthy right hand' as long as his voice would let him, and using while he could the words of Stephen, first martyr, 'Lord Jesus receive my spirit . . . I see heaven open and Jesus standing at the right hand of God.'

So it was that 'in the greatness of the flame, he gave up the ghost'.

The repercussions of that rainy Saturday have spread through the centuries like the ripples of a stone thrown into the pool of history. But in Oxford it was not until three centuries later that the Oxford martyrs were commemorated in Gilbert Scott's Martyrs' Memorial in St Giles. On it we read the following stark inscription:

To the Glory of God, and in grateful commemoration of His servants, Thomas Cranmer, Nicholas Ridley, Hugh Latimer, Prelates of the Church of England, who near this spot yielded their bodies to be burned, bearing witness to the sacred truths which they had affirmed and maintained against the errors of the Church of Rome, and rejoicing that to them it was given not only to believe in Christ, but also to suffer for His sake; this monument was erected by public subscription in the year of our Lord God, MDCCCXLI.

# 8

## *Edmund Campion*

*'Sufferings gladly born for others convert more people than sermons.' Thérèse de Lisieux*

Just a few yards from my home in Oxford is a yellow stone seminary, into the door of which is chiselled the name Campion Hall. I remember Edmund Campion often as I walk past that door. Thinking of his loving life is again to enter onto holy ground. He was indeed 'one of the great Elizabethans yet holy as none other of them'. And yet he was led out to his death not as a Protestant but as a Catholic; not under Mary but under Elizabeth, and no doubt much against her will. For the tide had turned back once again in Reformation England.

I include him here because of his courage and Christlikeness. I sometimes reflect on how he would have conversed with those other godly Oxford martyrs who died for another cause, namely to rid England of Roman heresy. Campion died to restore it, or to restore the Church, or indeed as he put it, 'to win you to heaven'.

Certainly when Latimer, Ridley and Cranmer, to say

nothing of Bilney and Tyndale before them, went to their doom, they did so for a cause: that of the apostolic preaching of the cross. They knew that faith in Christ's sacrifice, once for all, alone gives access to heaven and the Father's love. As Bilney said of the discovery of St Paul and justification by faith,

> Immediately I felt a marvelous comfort and quietness insomuch that my bruised bones leapt for joy . . . I learnt that all my travails, all my fasting and watching, all the redemption of masses and pardons, being done without trust in Christ, who only saveth his people from their sins, these, I say, I learnt to be nothing else but even . . . a hasty running out of the right way.[1]

Edmund Campion, who certainly trusted in Christ but understood his Church differently, was born in London on the 25th January 1540. He was 16 when Cranmer went to the stake in 1556. When Mary Tudor entered London in state as queen, he was the schoolboy chosen to give the Latin greeting to Her Majesty. Sir Thomas White, lord mayor, who built and endowed St John's College at Oxford, accepted Campion as one of his first scholars, appointing him junior fellow at the age of 17. Campion shone at Oxford and for twelve years he was to be followed and imitated as no man ever was in an English university except himself and John Henry Newman.[2] He took both his degrees and became a celebrated tutor. By 1568, he was junior proctor.

Queen Elizabeth had visited Oxford two years before. Won over by Campion's bearing, beauty and wit, she made him ask for whatever preferment he wanted. He took the Oath of Supremacy, submitting to Elizabeth as head of the

Church. But afterthoughts developed into scruples, scruples into anguish, and he broke off his happy Oxford life when his proctorship ended and moved to Ireland. He crossed to England in disguise and reached London in time to witness the trial of one of the earliest Oxford Catholic martyrs under Elizabeth, Dr John Storey.

Campion now recognised his calling to the priesthood and moved to the Catholic seminary at Douai. Thus began the exile of 'one of the diamonds of England'.[3] From Douai Campion set out as a barefoot pilgrim to Rome, where he became a Jesuit. The Society of Jesus (SJ) had only been in existence for 33 years. At worst, the Jesuits were to become the perpetrators of the dreaded terror of the Inquisition. At best, they were a missionary society dedicated to the imitation of Jesus. This is Evelyn Waugh's description of them at the time:

> The Society knew no bounds for its work but those of the human race; its missionaries penetrated to India, China, Japan, Abyssinia and the New World; in the lecture halls of the ancient universities, in obscure provincial day schools, guarding the consciences of great ladies at court and of dying seamen on the bullet-swept decks at Lepanto, among galley-slaves and lepers, in council with Cardinals and men of affairs, wherever souls were to be saved, these men of single purpose were making a way.[4]

Campion's call to this mission is reminiscent of others who 'left the world'. Of his decision to join the Jesuits, he writes to a friend who provided accommodation at that time:

> Did you not spend your entire self on me? One from whom there could be no repayment, *one just embarking from the world,*

*in some sort a dying man.* It is a work of high compassion to bury
the dead. You were munificent to me as I went to my rest in
the sepulchre of the Church.[5]

In his 'Brag' quoted at the end of this chapter, he speaks of
'being now as a dead man to this world and willing to put
my head under every man's foot'.

He moved to Prague, and there he was ordained in 1578.
Meanwhile, the so-called 'apostolic work of the English
mission' was being organised. In the garden of his monastery, Campion had a vision in which he was told of his
martyrdom. Friends at Prague were moved to make a scroll
for 'Edmund Campion, Martyr', and to paint a prophetic
garland of roses within his cell.

When he arrived in secret in London, his job was chiefly
to reclaim Catholics who were wavering under govern-
mental pressure; but his zeal to win Protestants, his preaching, his whole saintly and soldierly personality, made a
general and profound impression. An alarm was raised and
he fled to the north. Tracts appeared against him, such as
one entitled 'An answer to a seditious pamphlet lately put
about by a Jesuit', which gave six arguments insisting that
the Church of Rome was the Antichrist because they 'cru-
cify the Son of God again and again in their most blasphemous sacrifice of the Mass'.

Campion replied with his famous 'Ten Reasons'. This
consisted of ten reasons why the Protestants were wrong
in their argument. Campion's original title was 'Heresy in
Despair'. Its shining prose showed just how dangerous he
was to Elizabeth, who had chosen the other side. It was not
so much that Campion wanted to overthrow Elizabeth, but

he did believe in the supremacy of the Pope, which inevitably undermined Elizabeth even though he insisted it did not.

Thus the complexities of politics and power, as so often, mingled with courageous calling. In the end a spy, one George Eliot, was hot upon Campion's track, and ran him and others down at Lyford Grange near Wantage in Berkshire on the 17th July 1581.

Amid scenes of violent excitement, Campion was derisively paraded through the streets of his native city, bound hand and foot, riding backwards, with a paper stuck in his hat to denote the 'seditious Jesuit'. First thrown into the Tower, he was carried privately to the house of his old patron, the Earl of Leicester. There he encountered the queen herself, and 'received earnest proffers of liberty and preferments would he only give up his papistry'.[6]

On Campion's return to the Tower, he was examined under torture. He had asked for a public debate. But when it came off in the Norman chapel of the Tower, before the Dean of St Paul's and other divines, Campion had been denied opportunity to prepare his debate, and had been severely stretched on the rack. Thus weakened, he stood through the four long conferences, without chair, table or notes, and for Catholic commentators he 'stood undefeated'.[7]

A trial ensued in Westminster Hall on the 20th November 1581. Campion, pleading not guilty, was quite unable to hold up his often-wrenched right arm, seeing which a fellow prisoner, first kissing it, raised it for him. He made a magnificent defence. But the sentence was death, by hanging, drawing and quartering: a sentence received by the martyr with a joyful shout of '*Te Deum*!' Campion was dragged to Tyburn on the 1st December. On the scaffold, when interrupted and taunted to express his mind concerning the Bull of Excommunication of Elizabeth, he answered only by a prayer for her, 'your Queen and my Queen'. He was a Catholic Englishman with political opinions which were for the primacy of the Pope but also for the reign of Elizabeth. The people loudly lamented his fate, and a harvest of conversions to Catholicism began. A wild, generous-hearted youth called Henry Walpole, standing by, got his white doublet stained with Campion's blood. The incident made him, too, in time, a martyr.

Historians of all schools praise his high intelligence, his beautiful gaiety, his fiery energy, his chivalrous gentleness. He had renounced all opportunity for a dazzling career in the world of men. Every tradition of Edmund Campion, every remnant of his written words, shows us that he was nothing less than a man of genius, 'truly one of the great Elizabethans, but holy as none other of them all'.

I include Campion in this series of sketches of those whose passion shaped nations because he certainly contributed to the preservation of the witness in England of that great branch of the Church which is the Catholic tradition. In recent years, the evangelical and influential Lausanne Congress on World Evangelisation has produced the memorable goal of 'Calling the whole Church to preach the whole gospel to the whole world in our generation'. England certainly needs the witness of the whole Church, including the Catholic Church, and Campion has helped us to benefit from it.

I include him also because of his combination of clarity and courage. He is an Elizabethan writer after the manner of Shakespeare and I conclude with extracts from his tract 'Campion's Brag'. This was published in advance of his arrest, and is addressed 'To the Right Honourable, The Lords of Her Majesty's Privy Council':

> Right Honourable:
> Whereas I have come out of Germany and Bohemia, being sent by my Superiors, and adventured myself into this noble Realm, my dear Country, for the glory of God and benefit of souls, I thought it like enough that, in this busy, watchful and suspicious world, I should either sooner or later be intercepted and stopped of my course. Wherefore, providing for all events, and uncertain what may become of me, when God shall haply deliver my body into durance, I supposed it needful to put this writing in a readiness, desiring your good Lordships to give it your reading, for to know my cause. This doing, I trust I shall ease you of some labour. For that which otherwise you must have sought for by practice of wit, I do now lay into your hands by plain confession.

He then describes how he is a priest, a Jesuit, and the fact that he has been sent to England to preach the gospel, administer the sacraments and bring instruction, and to refute errors, 'in brief, to cry alarm spiritual against foul vice and proud ignorance, wherewith many my dear Countrymen are abused'.

Campion insists on his loyalty to Elizabeth:

> I never had mind, and am strictly forbidden by our Father that sent me, to deal in any respect with matter of State or Policy of this realm, as things which appertain not to my vocation, and from which I do gladly restrain and sequester my thoughts.

He then turns to the logic of his case for Catholicism:

I would be loath to speak anything that might sound of any insolent brag or challenge, especially being now as a dead man to this world and willing to put my head under every man's foot . . . Yet have I such a courage in avouching the Majesty of Jesus my King, and such assurance in my quarrel, and my evidence so impregnable, and because I know perfectly that no one Protestant, nor all the Protestants living . . . can maintain their doctrine in disputation. I am to sue most humbly and instantly for the combat with all and every of them. . .

He goes on to plead for an audience:

And because it hath pleased God to enrich the Queen my Sovereign Lady with notable gifts of nature, learning, and princely education, I do verily trust that – if her Highness would vouchsafe her royal person and good attention to such a conference . . . such manifest and fair light by good method and plain dealing may be cast upon these controversies, that possibly her zeal of truth and love of her people shall incline her noble Grace to disfavour some proceedings hurtful to the Realm, and procure towards us oppressed more equity.

He now appeals to the heart in perhaps his most famous paragraph:

Many innocent hands are lifted up to heaven for you daily by those English students, whose posterity shall never die, which beyond seas, gathering virtue and sufficient knowledge for the purpose, are determined never to give you over, but either to win you heaven, or to die upon your pikes. And touching our Society, be it known to you that we have made a league – all the Jesuits in the world, whose succession and multitude must overreach all the practices of England – cheerfully to carry the cross you shall lay upon us, and never to despair your recovery, while we have a man left to enjoy your Tyburn, or to be racked with your torments, or consumed with your prisons. The expense is reckoned, the enterprise is begun; it is of God, it cannot be withstood. So the faith was planted: so it must be restored.

What is remarkable about these paragraphs is the conciliatory, appeasing, yet sharply persuasive tone. It does remind us of Paul in its appeal to love, reason, revelation and, finally, to a heavenly perspective which 'loves not the world'. The word to describe him is indeed a 'diamond' in that he is clear, shining and sharp, even cutting. This is how he concludes and this is how we will leave him:

If these my offers be refused, and my endeavours can take no place, and I, having run thousands of miles to do you good, shall be rewarded with rigour, I have no more to say but to recommend your case and mine to Almighty God, the Searcher of Hearts, who send us His grace, and set us at accord before the day of payment, to the end we may at last be friends in heaven, when all injuries shall be forgotten.[8]

# 9

# James Hannington and the Uganda Martyrs

*'Tell the king that I die for Uganda. I have bought this road with my life.' James Hannington*

Among the statues of the ten martyrs over the West Door of Westminster Abbey in London, Ugandan Archbishop Janani Luwum finds his rightful place, along with his statement, 'I am prepared to die in the arms of Jesus.'[1] Janani was arrested and killed under the terrifying reign of Idi Amin that plunged Uganda into a chaos from which she is only just emerging. But Luwum was in fact one in a line of martyrs who gave their lives so that Uganda might know Christ. The first is commemorated in the stained-glass window of St Aldate's, Oxford, where I serve. His name is James Hannington.

For Hannington, it all began with a letter to the *Daily Telegraph* from Mutesa I, King of Buganda, asking for help to bring light to a country which was, according to the king, 'in total darkness'. James Hannington was quick to respond. Already in fact the gospel had got to Uganda and Hannington was, as so often is the case, joining in with what the Holy Spirit was already doing.

James Hannington was born the son of a merchant on the 3rd September 1847. His grandfather, Smith Hannington, was the founder of Hanningtons, Brighton's erstwhile leading department store. As a young man he worked in his father's business, until the late 1860s. James Hannington did not consider himself a hero. Yet it is impossible for us to view him in any other light.

After an adventurous childhood (which included blowing off his thumb with black powder) he received a bachelor's degree from Oxford in 1873 and was ordained by the Church of England. Although highly successful with his church work, in 1882 he was sent by the Church Missionary Society to the Lake Victoria region of Africa. His first attempt to reach that part of Africa failed. Consumed by fevers, he often had to be carried. When he walked, he tied his hands around his neck to relieve the agony in his arms. Yet he made humorous sketches of his plight.

The nineteenth century was the century of missionary expansion. Fired by a passion to share the good news of God in Christ, missionaries pushed through African jungles and deserts, the forbidden 10/40 window of their day. They learned languages, and braved pestilential climates to create schools, hospitals and churches. Some were killed, others contracted debilitating diseases, but by the century's end a global missionary presence was in place. The picture of missionary expansion was by no means a triumphal journey. Disease and martyrdom claimed great numbers. James Hannington became Bishop of Eastern Equatorial Africa in 1884 at the age of 37 and began his tragic voyage towards Uganda.

Influences struggling to hold sway at King Mutesa's court came from the Arabs (Muslims), the Catholics (the French, or *Bafaransa*) and the Protestants (the English, or *Bangereza*).

Mutesa let his subjects of all ranks join any creed of their choice. There was a competitive struggle for the soul of Uganda. Christianity was received with much excitement, but it came with its own requirements. It required a radical break with the old lifestyle. The new flock of believers (*abasomi*, or readers, as they were called) were therefore seemingly regarded as 'rebels' who had transferred their loyalty to the new religious system, thus abandoning the old tribal traditions.

Mutesa had astuteness and maturity in dealing with influences on his court. But he never committed himself to any of them. He died still a traditionalist. It is an irony that this very political indecision may have contributed to the holocaust unleashed by his nervy son Mwanga when the heir became king. Although Mwanga had shown some love for the missionaries as a young prince, his attitude changed on his accession. The once lively supporter became a vicious, intolerant persecutor of Christians and all foreigners. He felt (reasonably) that the converts had diverted their loyalty to some other allegiance. By the time Hannington arrived on the edge of Uganda, hardly a year after Mwanga's coronation, the king had already ordered the execution of the first three Christian martyrs, who died in January 1885. This was the ominous backdrop to Hannington's arrival.

Hannington tried approaching Uganda from the northeast. This proved to be a mistake. Uganda's suspicious king lumped him in with the Germans, who were grabbing territory in that direction. He sent a thousand Ugandan soldiers to intercept Hannington. On the 21st October 1885, they took him prisoner. They allowed him a little freedom at first and he walked out to look at the Nile. We know most of this detail because one of the Ugandans kept Hannington's journal and sold it to a later expedition. His journal tells what happened next:

Suddenly about twenty ruffians set upon us. They violently threw me to the ground, and proceeded to strip me of all valuables. Thinking they were robbers I shouted for help, when they forced me up and hurried me away, as I thought, to throw me down a precipice close at hand. I shouted again in spite of one threatening to kill me with a club. Twice I nearly broke away from them, and then grew faint with struggling and was dragged by the legs over the ground. I said, 'Lord, I put myself in Thy hands, I look to Thee alone.' Then another struggle and I got to my feet and was then dashed along. More than once I was violently brought into contact with banana trees, some trying in their haste to force me one way, others the other, and the exertion and struggling strained me in the most agonizing manner. In spite of all, and feeling I was being dragged away to be murdered at a distance, I sang 'Safe in the Arms of Jesus' and laughed at the very agony of my situation. My clothes were torn to pieces so that I was exposed; wet through with being dragged on the ground; strained in every limb, and for a whole hour expecting instant death, hurried along, dragged, pushed at five miles an hour, until we came to a hut. . .

Hannington wrote on the 22nd October:

The outlook is gloomy . . . Starvation, desertion, treachery, and a few other nightmares and furies hover over one's head in ghostly forms, and yet in spite of it all, I feel in capital spirits. Let me beg every mite of spare prayer. You must uphold my hands, lest they fall. If this is the last chapter of earthly history, then the next will be the first page of the heavenly – no blots and smudges, no incoherence, but sweet converse in the presence of the Lamb.

He was held prisoner by a regional ruler near the Uganda border and wrote:

> 28th (7th day). A terrible night; first with noisy, drunken guards, and secondly with vermin, which have found out my tent and swarm. I don't think I got one hour's sleep, and woke with fever fast developing. O Lord, do have mercy on me, and release me! I am quite broken down and brought low. Comforted by reading 27th Psalm. Fever developed very rapidly . . . soon was delirious. Evening. Fever passed away. Word came that Mwanga had sent three soldiers, but what news they bring they will not yet let me know. Much comforted by the 28th Psalm.
>
> 29th (8th day). I can hear no news, but was held up by the 30th Psalm, which came with great power. A hyena howled near me last night, smelling a sick man. I hope it is not to have me yet.

So it was that the bishop and his 50 porters were led out and killed. His last words are reported to have been, 'Tell the king that I die for Uganda. I have bought this road with my life.' It is recorded that on his march to martyrdom he sang the new song 'Safe in the Arms of Jesus', written by Fanny Crosby in the 1860s. We produce it here to try to catch some of Hannington's courage and his hope and safety in Christ.

> Safe in the arms of Jesus, safe on His gentle breast,
> There by His love o'er shaded, sweetly my soul shall rest.
> Hark! 'tis the voice of angels, borne in a song to me,
> Over the fields of glory, over the jasper sea.
>
> Safe in the arms of Jesus, safe from corroding care,
> Safe from the world's temptations, sin cannot harm me there.
> Free from the blight of sorrow, free from my doubts and fears;
> Only a few more trials, only a few more tears.
>
> Jesus, my heart's dear refuge, Jesus had died for me;
> Firm on the Rock of Ages, ever my trust shall be.

Here let me wait with patience, wait till the night is o'er;
Wait till I see the morning break on the golden shore.

*Refrain*:
Safe in the arms of Jesus, safe on His gentle breast,
There by His love o'er shaded, sweetly my soul shall rest.

Widespread persecution of Christians followed, many being killed or sold to Arab slavers. Joseph Mukasa, senior advisor to the king and a Catholic convert, criticised Mwanga for ordering Hannington's death without giving him a chance to defend himself as was their custom. On the 15th November Mukasa was arrested and became the first Catholic martyr. Between December 1885 and May 1886 many more converts were murdered. Mwanga precipitated a showdown by ordering the converts to choose between their new faith and complete obedience to his orders. Those unwilling to obey in all things would be put to death. It is a remarkable fact that the Christians, often teenagers, chose death, which usually came by burning.

For Mwanga it is said that the ultimate humiliation from his pages was when they resisted his homosexual advances. According to old tradition the king was the centre of power and he could dispense it as he saw fit. There is an old expression in Luganda: *Namunswa alya kunswase* ('the queen ant feeds on her subjects'). Although homosexuality is abhorred among the Baganda, it was equally unheard of for pages to resist the wishes of their king. It is alleged that Mwanga learnt or acquired homosexual behaviour from the Arabs.[2] Given this conflict, he determined to rid his realm of these Christians.[3] This version of events is to be found whenever Christians tell the story. For example, it was

remembered by Sandy Millar at the time of the enthrone-
ment of Henry Orombi as the new Archbishop of Uganda, a
service at which Sandy preached.[4] It was told to me when
we last visited the martyrs' memorial at Namugongo Theological College, which commemorates the 45 known Protestant and Catholic martyrs who could be formally accounted
for. We were told that the king challenged the pages: 'Does
not your faith tell you that you should obey your king in all
things?' To which their reply was simply, 'We have heard
that there is a King of kings and we must follow him.'

We were also told, during the hushed narrative from a
godly guide that day, of the way in which the martyrs were
trussed and bound up in rush mats and fed onto the fire like
so many logs, but that they testified loudly to the 'coolness
of the flames and to the waterfall that refreshed them as
they died'. This vision or reality is recorded in the wall-sized
mural in the large hall of the college, along with the letter
of King Mutesa to the *Telegraph*, the arrival and martyrdom
of Hannington, the burnings and persecution, and then the
extraordinary growth of Christianity that ensued. For, as so
often, the 'blood of the martyrs is the seed of the Church'.
In his efforts to curb the Christian influence, the king found
he had made another of history's great miscalculations. The
Namugongo martyrdoms produced a result entirely opposite
to Mwanga's intentions. The example of these martyrs, who
walked to their deaths singing hymns and praying for their
enemies, so inspired many of the bystanders that they
began to seek instruction from the remaining Christians.
Within a few years the original handful of converts had
multiplied many times and spread far beyond the court. The
martyrs had left the indelible impression that Christianity

was truly African, not simply a white man's religion. Most of the missionary work was carried out by Africans rather than by white missionaries, and Christianity spread steadily. Uganda now has the largest percentage of professed Christians of any nation in Africa.

Renewed persecution of Christians in the 1970s by the military dictatorship of Idi Amin proved the vitality of the example of the Namugongo martyrs. Among the thousands of new martyrs, both Anglican and Roman, was Janani Luwum, Archbishop of the (Anglican) Church of Uganda.

In 1971 Milton Obote, prime minister of Uganda, was overthrown by General Idi Amin, chief of staff of the armed forces. Almost immediately he began a policy of repression, arresting anyone suspected of not supporting him. Hundreds of soldiers from the Lango and Acholi tribes were shot down in their barracks. Amin ordered the expulsion of the Asian population of Uganda, about 55,000 people, mostly shopkeepers from India and Pakistan. Over the next few years, many Christians were killed for various offences. A preacher who read on the radio a psalm which mentioned Israel was shot for this in 1972. It was in the midst of such a society that Luwum was elected Archbishop of Uganda in 1974. Amin determined to stamp out all traces of dissent. His men killed thousands, including the entire population of Milton Obote's home village.

On Sunday the 30th January 1976 Bishop Festo Kivengere preached on 'The Preciousness of Life' to an audience including many high government officials. He denounced the arbitrary bloodletting and accused the government of abusing the authority that God had entrusted to it. The government responded on the following Saturday (5th

February) by an early morning raid on the home of the Archbishop, Janani Luwum, ostensibly to search for hidden stores of weapons. The Archbishop called on President Amin to deliver a note of protest at the policies of arbitrary killings and the unexplained disappearances of many persons. Church leaders were summoned to Kampala and then ordered to leave, one by one. Luwum turned to Festo Kivengere and said, 'They are going to kill me. I am not afraid.'

Amin accused Luwum of treason, produced a document supposedly by former President Obote attesting his guilt, and had the Archbishop and two Cabinet members (both committed Christians) arrested and held for military trial. The three met briefly with four other prisoners who were awaiting execution, and were permitted to pray with them. Then the three were placed in a Land Rover and were not seen alive again by their friends. The government story is that one of the prisoners tried to seize control of the vehicle and that it was wrecked and the passengers killed. The story believed by the Archbishop's supporters is that he refused to sign a confession, was beaten and otherwise abused, and finally shot. His body was placed in a sealed coffin and sent to his native village for burial. However, the villagers opened the coffin and discovered the bullet holes. In the capital city of Kampala a crowd of about 4,500 gathered for a memorial service beside the grave that had been prepared for him next to that of the martyred Bishop Hannington. In Nairobi, the capital of nearby Kenya, about 10,000 gathered for another memorial service. Bishop Kivengere was informed that he was about to be arrested, and he and his family fled to Kenya, as did the widow and children of Archbishop Luwum.

The following June, about 25,000 Ugandans came to the

capital to celebrate the centennial of the first preaching of the gospel in their country. Among the participants were many who had abandoned Christianity, but who had returned to their faith as a result of seeing the courage of Archbishop Luwum and his companions in the face of death. Uganda, once described by Churchill as 'the pearl of Africa', still struggles to fulfil its destiny. It has fought through Amin's oppression, the AIDS epidemic and now the genocide and terror of the 'Lord's Resistance Army' in the north of the country. And yet scenes of revival, a deep and life-changing prayer awakening, continue to make Uganda a place of hope for the whole African continent. The current Christian church has its eye not only on the conversion of individuals but also on the very transformation of society. We can learn from this in praying for nations; we can remember John Knox's statement, 'Give me Scotland or I die.' In Uganda, the blood of the martyrs does not seem to have been shed in vain.

The Anglican Church, of which Hannington was a bishop, uses this prayer to commemorate his death:

Precious in your sight, O Lord, is the death of your saints, whose faithful witness, by your providence, has its great reward: We give you thanks for your martyrs James Hannington and his companions, who purchased with their blood a road to Uganda for the proclamation of the gospel; and we pray that with them we also may obtain the crown of righteousness which is laid up for all who love the appearing of our Saviour Jesus Christ; who lives and reigns with you and the Holy Spirit, one God, for ever and ever. Amen.

# 10

## *Dietrich Bonhoeffer and Paul Schneider*

*'I believe that unarmed truth and unconditional love will have the final word in reality. That is why right, temporarily defeated, is stronger than evil triumphant.' Martin Luther King*[1]

*'I have already noticed that here, where all comfort is taken away, the soul becomes much hungrier, and God's word sinks much deeper into it.' Paul Schneider*[2]

'When Christ calls a man', says Dietrich Bonhoeffer, 'he bids him come and die.' There are different kinds of dying, it is true; but the essence of discipleship is contained in these words ... Dietrich himself was a martyr many times before he died. He was one of the bravest witnesses against idolatry. He understood what he chose when he chose resistance ... From him more than any other German, I learnt the true character of the conflict, in an intimate friendship ... He was completely regardless of personal safety, while deeply moved by the shame of the country he loved. Wherever he went, he was undaunted, detached from himself, devoted to his friends, to his home, to his country as God meant it to be, to his Church, to his Master.

These words by Bishop Bell from the foreword to Bonhoeffer's masterly book *Nachfolge* (literally 'following after' but translated 'the cost of discipleship') introduce us to someone who not only went to his death because of his witness to Christ, but who thought and wrote deeply about that cost.[3]

Bonhoeffer – along with his twin sister Sabine – was born on the 4th February 1906 in Breslau, Germany. His parents, outstanding in character, introduced him to that Christian humanitarianism that 'was as native as the air they breathed'.[4] All testify to this being a jewel of a man. His love of the arts, music, the mountains, the flowers, the animals, his readiness to listen and his firm character made him a man of many friends. But he was also marked by his unselfish readiness to help others to the point of sacrifice. Bonhoeffer was ready where others were not to take the risk of tasks that required special courage. Later a student in Tübingen, Berlin, and at Union Theological Seminary in New York, as well as a participant in the European ecumenical movement, Bonhoeffer became known as one of the few figures of the 1930s with a comprehensive grasp of both German- and English-language theology. His works resonate with a prescience, subtlety and maturity that continually belie the youth of their author.

Bonhoeffer received his doctorate from Berlin University in 1927 and lectured in the theological faculty during the early 1930s. He was ordained a Lutheran pastor in 1931 and served two Lutheran congregations, St Paul's and Sydenham, in London, from 1933 to 1935. A career in theological scholarship opened up to him, as his *Ethics* and *On Community* show, but he willingly laid it down. For God had chosen for him this path of downward mobility, of giving up his life, of martyrdom. '"Do you seek great things for yourself? Seek them not. For I will bring disaster on all people." I can't get away from Jeremiah 45,' he wrote from prison. He was one of few who understood, even before Hitler came to power, that National Socialism was a brutal attempt to make history without God. He saw Nazism as a counter-religion and a danger to Christianity. As late as 1933, he spoke on the radio against a political system which misled its people and made of its Führer an idol and even God.

He realised that nothing was to be gained by the churches reciting their old credal statements. The desire for a new start and new orientation led him to seek relationship with other world churches, and to involvement in the new ecumenical movement. In 1934, 2,000 Lutheran pastors organised the Pastors' Emergency League in opposition to the state church controlled by the Nazis. This organisation evolved into the Confessing Church, a free and independent Protestant church. Bonhoeffer served as head of the Confessing Church's illegal seminary at Finkenwalde. Here he wrote the haunting *On Community*, so often quoted by British evangelist David Watson and his many disciples as he sought to build a completely new form of church in the 1970s and 80s, a legacy that is with us to this day. Bonhoeffer was the author of pithy aphoristic and unforgettable phrases, such as 'He who loves his dream of Community more than the community itself will destroy the latter,' or 'The Church has an unconditional obligation to the victims of any ordering of society. There are things for which an uncompromising stand is worthwhile.'[5] His attempt to build community in the gathering darkness of 1930s Germany is no doubt prophetic for our age. Likewise his emphasis on 'discipleship taking form within a band of men'. The activities of the Confessing Church were virtually outlawed and its five seminaries closed by the Nazis in 1937. Interestingly, Bonhoeffer safely escaped the troubles in Europe and went to teach in New York in June 1939. But he returned abruptly less than a month later, saying:

I have had time to think and to pray about my situation, and that of my nation, and to have God's will for me clarified. I have come to the conclusion that I have made a mistake in coming to America. I shall have no right to participate in the reconstruction of the Christian life in Germany after the war if I did not share in the trials of this time with my people. Christians in Germany face the terrible alternative of willing the defeat of their nation in order that civilization may survive, or willing the victory of their nation and thereby destroying civilization. I know which of these alternatives I must choose. But I cannot make that choice in security.

Bonhoeffer's active opposition to National Socialism in the 1930s continued to escalate until his recruitment into the resistance in 1940. The core of the conspiracy to assassinate Adolf Hitler and overthrow the Third Reich was an elite group within the Abwehr (German Military Intelligence) which included Admiral Wilhelm Canaris, Head of Military Intelligence, General Hans Oster, who recruited Bonhoeffer, and Hans von Dohnanyi, who was married to Bonhoeffer's sister Christine. Bonhoeffer's role in the conspiracy was that of courier and diplomat to the British government on behalf of the resistance, since Allied support was essential to stopping the war. Between trips abroad for the resistance, Bonhoeffer stayed at Ettal, a Benedictine monastery outside Munich, where he worked on his book *Ethics* from 1940 until his arrest in 1943. Bonhoeffer, in effect, was formulating the ethical basis for a situation in which the performance of certain extreme actions, such as political assassination, was required of a morally responsible person, while at the same time attempting to overthrow the Third Reich in what everyone expected to be a very bloody coup d'état.

This combination of action and thought qualifies as one of the more unique moments in intellectual history. His participation in the murder plot delivered Bonhoeffer from his perhaps natural position as a pacifist. His sister-in-law, Emmi Bonhoeffer, cited his reasoning. He told her, 'If I see a madman driving a car into a group of innocent by-standers, then I can't, as a Christian, simply wait for the catastrophe and then comfort the wounded and bury the dead. I must try to wrestle the steering wheel out of the hands of the driver.'

He was arrested and imprisoned on the 5th April 1943 at the age of 37 and taken to Tegel Prison, Berlin. On the 7th February 1945 he was moved to Buchenwald Concentration Camp. Bonhoeffer, even while in prison, maintained his pastoral role. Those who were with him spoke of the guidance and spiritual inspiration he gave, not only to fellow inmates but to prison guards as well. In a letter smuggled out of prison, he showed no bitterness but rather explained how 'we in the resistance have learned to see the great events of world history from below, from the perspective of the excluded, the ill treated, the powerless, the oppressed and despised . . . so that personal suffering has become a more useful key for understanding the world than personal happiness'.

He had already worked this out in theory when he wrote *The Cost of Discipleship*. Here we can almost hear him preaching to and preparing his students for the days ahead:

> The cross is laid on every Christian. The first Christ-suffering which every man must experience is the call to abandon the attachments of this world. It is that dying of the old man which is the result of his encounter with Christ. As we embark upon discipleship, we surrender our lives to Christ in union with his death: we give our lives over to death. Thus it begins: the cross is not the terrible end to an otherwise god-fearing and happy life, but it meets us at the beginning of our communion with Christ. When Christ calls a man, he bids him come and die . . . But how will the disciple know what kind of cross is meant for him? He will find out as soon as he begins to follow his Lord and share his life.
>
> Suffering then is the badge of true discipleship. The disciple is not above his master. Following Christ means 'passio passiva', suffering because we have to suffer. This is why Luther reckoned suffering among the marks of the true Church, and one of the suggestions drawn up for the Augsburg Confession defines the Church as the community of 'those who are persecuted and martyred for the gospel's sake'. The opposite of discipleship is to be ashamed of Christ and his cross and all the offence the cross brings in its train.
>
> Discipleship means allegiance to the suffering Christ and it is therefore not at all surprising that Christians should be called upon to suffer. It is a joy and a token of his grace. The acts of the early Christian martyrs are full of evidence which shows how Christ transfigures for his own the hour of their agony by granting them the unspeakable assurance of his presence. In the

hour of cruellest suffering they bear for his sake, they are made partakers in the perfect joy and bliss of fellowship with him.[6]

On Christmas Eve 1943, in the Gestapo prison in Berlin, he wrote a revealing letter to his friends Eberhard and Renate Bethge. Eberhard was expecting to be drafted into the German Wehrmacht (the army), to a war that was already lost.

> Dear Eberhard, Dear Renate: . . .I've had a few lovely hours of peace and quiet . . . I wish I could say something to help you in this time of separation . . . I have learned something about it myself during the last nine months, having been separated during that time from all those I love . . . Nothing can fill the gap when we are away from those we love. And it would be wrong to try to find anything. We must simply hold on and win through. That sounds very hard at first, but at the same time, it is a great consolation, since leaving the gap unfilled preserves the bonds between us. It is nonsense to say that God fills the gap: God does not fill it, but keeps it empty, so that our communication with one another may be kept alive, even at the cost of pain.[7]

His concern in prison was to get permission to minister to the sick and to his fellow prisoners. He impressed others deeply with his self-control during very heavy bombing of Berlin, when the explosions were accompanied by the howlings of other prisoners who beat on their cell doors, screaming to be taken to safety. Bonhoeffer stood like a giant, ministering peace and practical help. Yet there was another, weaker, all too human side to him, as is evidenced by his famous poem 'Who Am I?'.

> Who am I? They often tell me
> I would step from my cell's confinement

calmly, cheerfully, firmly,
like a squire from his country-house.

Who am I? They often tell me
I would talk to my warden
freely and friendly and clearly,
as though it were mine to command.

Who am I? They also tell me
I would bear the days of misfortune
equably, smilingly, proudly,
like one accustomed to win.

Am I then really all that which other men tell of, or am I only
what I know of myself, restless and longing and sick, like a bird
in a cage, struggling for breath, as though hands were com-
pressing my throat, yearning for colours, for flowers, for the
voices of birds, thirsting for words of kindness, for neighbourli-
ness, trembling with anger at despotisms and petty humiliation,
tossing in expectation of great events, powerlessly trembling
for friends at an infinite distance, weary and empty at praying,
at thinking, at making, faint and ready to say farewell to it all?

Who am I? This or the other?
Am I one person today, and tomorrow another?
Who am I? They mock me, these lonely questions of mine.
Whoever I am, Thou knowest, O God, I am Thine.[8]

What the prospect of death means to a church leader is
remote from the experience of most of us. But Bishop
Berggrav of Norway has written of his own experiences in
the modern church struggle, and shows us what we might
have guessed, that face to face with death there is neither
archbishop nor bishop, neither cleric nor layman, but only
the liberty of a Christian man.

A solicitor appeared in my cell . . . to tell me that it was decided that I should be shot on Monday. An arrow went through my heart of course, but once again I felt my safeguardedness in God, and when two days later the solicitor reappeared to tell me that the decision had to be altered I almost felt disappointed . . . so it was all the time . . . half your soul in anxiety of fear and doubt: the other half of your soul is in heaven, carried on the wings of faith which God bestows on you.[9]

Bonhoeffer's poem could be a commentary on Paul's thoughts to the Corinthians, when he speaks from prison about the position of the Christian who is at once part of the kingdom of God but at the same time not yet seeing it. This 'now and not yet' state is particularly acute for the Christian prisoner, of course. Paul sums it up:

. . .through glory and dishonour, bad report and good report; genuine, yet regarded as impostors; known, yet regarded as unknown; dying, and yet we live on; beaten, and yet not killed; sorrowful, yet always rejoicing; poor, yet making many rich; having nothing, and yet possessing everything. (2 Cor. 6:8–10)

On the 9th April 1945 Bonhoeffer, along with other members of the Admiral Canaris resistance group, was executed by hanging in Flossenburg Prison, where he had been transferred from Buchenwald. American troops were only miles away. Bonhoeffer's executioners entered his cell and led him to the gallows. He whispered to a fellow prisoner as he was being led away, 'This is the end, but for me, the beginning of life.'

He went calmly to his death. That morning as he was led out of his cell he was observed by the prison doctor, who said, 'Through the half-open door I saw Pastor Bonhoeffer still in his prison clothes, kneeling in fervent prayer to the Lord his God. The devotion and evident conviction of being heard that I saw in the prayer of this intensely captivating man moved me to the depths.' The prisoners were ordered to strip. Naked under the scaffold, Bonhoeffer knelt for one last time to pray. Five minutes later, he was dead.

In the same month that Bonhoeffer was hanged, on the 30th April 1945, Hitler committed suicide. Seven days later Germany surrendered.

Dietrich Bonhoeffer was one, perhaps the leading one, of hundreds of Christian martyrs who gave their lives during the holocaust that was Nazi Germany, to say nothing of the six million Jews against whom the rage of this demonic counter-religion was unfurled. We will mention just one other, Paul Schneider, 'simple pastor of the Reformed tradition',[10] who became the 'pastor of Buchenwald'. Schneider preceded Bonhoeffer into heaven by seven years, and he was a prophetic voice to German Christians when he was arrested for the first time as early as 1934. The incident shows how subtle is the path a Christian witness/martyr may be called to tread. The occasion was the funeral of a young man who was also a leading member of the Nazi party. Party members had bedecked the church with swastikas and pronounced in different speeches that the deceased had gone straight to enrol in the storm troops of heaven. Schneider gently corrected this, saying he 'was not sure there were storm troops in heaven, but God the Lord bless thy going out and thy coming in from this time forth and forevermore', and he called the people inside the church for the memorial service before God and his holy word. He was then publicly rebuked for his correction. He continued to stand firm and the next day was arrested. It was the first time the danger of National Socialism had been felt in the region and many who had followed the Nazis began to waver. It was the beginning of a compelling call to opposition to the counter-religion. But persecution was a direct result of Paul Schneider's stand. Were he to be quiet, he would be left alone; were he to stand, he knew he risked prison, though no one thought yet of death. Paul's wife recounts the evolution of her understanding:

> We did not often talk of the fear that gripped my heart. But one day we had a never-to-be-forgotten conversation. Two incidents made me speak. The one on a footpath, we overtook a man who soon fell into conversation with Paul. I knew his method of using such opportunities well to witness for his Lord. He seemed to me then like a man who knew that he had not much time left. Flames leapt up as out of a hidden fire. The second incident was at the edge of the woods where a gypsy encampment was pitched. The men lay round the fire. Paul went over to them and spoke to them with a sense of intense urgency. Paul did this quite naturally, without condescension, and placed before them the decisive question of accepting Christ.
>
> On the way back I used the moment we had alone to ask him to be careful. He replied that he could only promise not to seek martyrdom. But, whenever he was called to witness, he must witness, because on earth there is no other salvation for men than in Jesus Christ. My heart sank and I began to speak about his wife and children. That moment I can never forget. We stood on the stone bridge which led over the water. He looked at me with an indescribable look, straight in the eyes, and said: 'Do you think God gave me my children only that I might care for their outward needs to keep them strong in

body? Do they not depend on me also to care for their eternity? And my wife? Perhaps it is for you that I must suffer, perhaps in this way and in no other can you break through to true faith.' Silent and inwardly shaking we walked home. I can never forget.[11]

Paul's preaching has from now on a ring similar to that of Bonhoeffer. Here he is just before Easter in 1937:

How stupidly men ask today, in various ways, about the Church struggle: Isn't the Church almost quiet and in order again? Hasn't it nearly been settled? Yes, I think it has – so would the comfortable members of the Church like to think. They are already shocked at the struggle and suffering to which God has led us, and think it quite impossible for matters to go further. Insofar as they think that, they look round for every possible way out of this suffering and struggle. These are friends of the Church; but there are others, the enemies of the Church, who also seek to end the struggle. They reckon that our cause – the cause of Jesus Christ – is lost. They think they have only to get rid of a crowd of troublesome parsons and all will be quiet in the Church. Both of them, friends and enemies, are unable to see that, for the Evangelical Church, the way of death is the way of Jesus, the way of the cross, the way of life. A glance at Russia should teach us. There every outward form of organized church life is destroyed, the pastors have disappeared and almost all the church property is taken away. And yet there the Church of Jesus Christ lives more and perhaps grows stronger than it does here in Germany. It lives under the holy cross. Because of persecution, they gather together in one another's houses, where lay-preachers declare the word of God and willingly take upon themselves the punishments of the law. Why then should not the way of the Church in Germany lead by way of far greater suffering and death through total defeat, to victory and to glory? Don't be deceived: you can have no part in the glory of Jesus or his victory, unless you are ready to take upon yourself the holy cross and with him tread the way of suffering and death. For that, faith is needed, a faith which knows the power and the victory of the cross. Such a faith is indeed a hidden and a quiet power. . .[12]

Schneider began to stand bravely and carefully for Christ, and these little acts of standing against the regime led inevitably to his arrest and eventually to his death. At his arrest, it is touching to see the complicity and courage of his wife smuggling in with his washbag the verse, 'Rejoice that your name is written in heaven.' She remarks, 'That lit up his darkness for a while.' And no doubt it did. He writes:

> Today is the sixth Sunday of my imprisonment and I have had no opportunity to take part in a service. But that does not mean I have not worshipped. I have already noticed that here, where all comfort is taken away, the soul becomes much hungrier, and God's word sinks much deeper into it.[13]

He became the pastor of the prison, Buchenwald, to which he was eventually taken. His letters show a constant concern for those to whom he writes, and a love for his fellow prisoners, but little care for himself. Particularly they show his touching, strengthening love affair with his wife.

Things came to a head in the camp when an order came that all prisoners passing the Nazi flag should salute it by taking off their caps. Schneider declared that saluting the flag was an idolatry and refused to obey the order. One prisoner who had a grudge against him informed the authorities. Then began Paul Schneider's lonely path to suffering and death.

The camp clerk Herr Leikam takes up the story:

He was called to the SS and freely confessed his attitude. At first he received twenty five lashes and was then put into the dark cell. This meant solitary confinement and he remained in this cell till his death. There he told the SS exactly what the Christian attitude to Nazism was. He spoke freely and without fear. There was probably no other man in Germany who denounced the regime as fearlessly. He called the devil by his name: murderer, criminal, tyrant, monster. Because of this witness against Nazism, and he never failed to set it against the grace of Christ and call men to repentance, Schneider received in his body repeated and heavy tortures, humiliations and pains. All the ingenuity of Nazi sadism was used against him. Torture was alternated with good treatment and appeals to relax his strong opposition. Schneider was unmoved and he was tireless in calling out words of Scripture to his fellow-prisoners. Morning and evening, whenever his cell door was opened or he was taken out to fresh torment, his voice could be heard shouting aloud words of comfort and judgement from the Bible . . . One January morning in 1939, when two escaped prisoners had been brought back and killed, Paul Schneider could be heard clearly denouncing the murder: 'In the name of Jesus Christ, I witness against the murder of prisoners. . .'

The worst time for Schneider was in the early summer of 1939. For several days he was hung up, with his hands behind him and his body permanently bent. This devilish device caused him continuous pain. His suffering was borne nobly and he was greatly honoured in the camp. We saw in him the meaning of the words: 'My bonds in Christ are manifest in all the palace.'[14]

He was kept for over a year in solitary confinement until his killing on the 14th July 1939. He was 41 years old.

In a letter two weeks after his death, Karl Barth summed up for many the life of this twentieth-century martyr for the gospel:

> He is delivered, his faith has become sight, he has gone home. The crown of life crowns the true man even in death. His faithful witness has helped many to do and say what is right and God has honoured him in allowing him to suffer. The New Testament speaks of this honour of suffering. It is not for nothing. It is a signpost, pointing up higher, where honour is given and the crown of life is received.[15]

# 11

# *Chinese Christianity – Crucified with Christ*

*'Dear ones, I long for a sight of your dear faces, but I fear we shall not meet on earth. I am preparing for the end very quietly and calmly. The Lord is wonderfully near and will not fail me. I was very restless and excited when there seemed a chance of life, but God has taken away that feeling and I now pray for peace to meet the terrible end bravely. The pain will soon be over, and O the sweetness of the welcome above! My little baby will go with me. I think God will give him to me in heaven. I cannot imagine the saviour's welcome. O that will compensate for all these days of suspense . . . I do not regret coming to China but I am sorry I have done so little. My married life, two precious years, has been so very full of happiness. We will die together, my dear husband and I.'* Lizzie Attwater's last letter to her family from Fenchow, North Shansi, 3rd August 1900[1]

*'The Lord has honoured us by giving fellowship in His sufferings. Three times stoned, robbed of everything, even clothes, we know what hunger, thirst, weariness, nakedness are as never before, but also the sustaining grace of God and His peace, in a new and deeper sense than before . . . billow after billow has gone over me. Home gone. Not one memento of dear Maggie even. Penniless: wife and child gone to glory.*

*And now that you know the worst, Mother, I want to tell you
that the cross of Christ, that exceeding glory of the Father's
love, has brought continual comfort to my heart, so that not
one murmur has broken the peace within.' CIM missionary
E.J. Cooper, Lucheng, summer 1900*

*'Jail has become the helpful training centre for the Church in
China.' Samuel Lamb*[2]

The troubled, glorious, agonised fight for the soul of China reached its heart of darkness in 1900 during the Boxer rebellion. But ever since Christianity had come to this beautiful, so populous land, it had been undergoing baptisms of fire. News of Jesus Christ may have reached China as early as the first century. An eighth-century Nestorian Church leader claimed that the Magi, returning from Bethlehem, had brought the first news of Christ to China. In the 1300s Franciscan missionaries made China a longed-for goal, but they aroused Islamic opposition and Christianity was all but swept out of Asia amidst great bloodshed.[3] Jesuit influence in the seventeenth century almost convinced the Chinese emperor to make China a Catholic state, but the insistence of the Pope in 1724 that the emperor's ancestor worship was incompatible with Christianity provoked the banning of Christianity and the death of hundreds of Catholic missionaries.

The first Protestant missionary, Robert Morrison, went to China in 1807, working with the East India Company, but despite translating almost the entire Bible into Mandarin he made little progress. Missionary hero James Hudson Taylor arrived in 1853, returning in 1866 with 22 workers in 'utter weakness, overwhelmed at the immensity of the task before us'. In 1900, 56 of Hudson Taylor's missionaries were to be martyred as the fury of the Boxers fell on the Christians.

The Chinese view the nineteenth century as the most degrading and humiliating time in their long history. The Japanese, British, Dutch, Spanish, French, Portuguese, Russians and other countries had seized Chinese land by military power and were exploiting China for its wealth and natural resources. The issue of responsibility is touched upon in the report of martyrdoms issued in 1900 by the China Inland Mission.[4] It was in this atmosphere that the secret Chinese society known as the Boxers was born. Working behind the scenes, they grew rapidly in influence until they had members in every part of the country.

In the last few years of the nineteenth century, foreign missionary activity became more and more difficult, and Chinese Christians were persecuted and accused of being 'running dogs' for the Western imperialists. Something was about to erupt. In June 1900 one observer noted:

> Crazed mobs rampaged through the cities of north China, looting and burning churches and the homes of missionaries and Chinese Christians. They were led by bare-chested fanatics called Boxers who brandished long curving swords and cried for the heads and hearts of Christians and missionaries.[5]

For Paul Cohen, the Boxer episode has to do with themes still unresolved in Chinese cultural identity, encompassing a love-hate relationship to their own past and to their relationship with the West. 'As long as this ambivalence remains, the Boxers, because of the themes they evoke, are likely to continue their extraordinary life as a storehouse of symbol and myth.'[6]

Be that as it may, the Boxer episode provoked scenes of great violence. It is worth recording some details here to attempt to understand the struggle for China. According to eyewitnesses, Chinese Christians were forced to kneel and drink the blood of foreigners who had been beheaded. Some also had crosses burned into their foreheads. One Chinese Christian mother and her two children were kneeling before the executioner when a watcher suddenly ran and pulled the children back into the anonymity of the observing crowd. The mother went to her death because she would not deny Christ. The Boxer rebellion exploded in early 1900. A hundred times as many Chinese lost their lives as foreign missionaries. One pastor refused to deny his faith in Jesus Christ. The mob cut off his eyebrows, ears and lips. When he still remained uncooperative, the furious crowd cut out his heart and displayed it for the public.[7] His 14-year-old daughter followed in his footsteps. After watching her father choose a torturous death rather than betray the God he loved, she could only do the same. The details of these events are documented in several places and in particular in *By Their Blood*, by James and Marti Hefley. This book tells us that in 1900 in Tsun-hua, almost 170 Chinese had committed their lives to Jesus and become his followers. When the Boxers swept through their land intent on stamping out the 'White Devils', almost all were killed. When a pastor was tied to a pillar inside a pagan temple, he preached to his captors and friends all night. In the morning, 'a thousand-strong mob descended on him and literally tore out his heart'. The same crowd chopped the feet off a

Christian Chinese teacher who refused to renounce Christ, then ran a sword through her. Another teacher was burned alive as she shouted to her pupils, 'Keep the faith!'

When violence broke out in June, the missionary compounds in Taiyuan were set on fire. The believers, Chinese and Western together, linked hands and sought temporary refuge in a Baptist boys' school. One missionary realised that two Chinese girls had been left behind, so she ran back to rescue them. The girls had managed to escape from their building, but the mob forced the lone missionary back into the blazing house. The girls she came to save watched her kneel in the midst of the flames.

Caught in Peking, Dr G.E. Morrison filed this report for the *London Times*:

As darkness came on the most awful cries were heard in the city, most demoniacal and unforgettable, the cries of the Boxers – *Sha kuei-tzu* [kill the devils] – mingled with the shrieks of the victims and the groans of the dying. For Boxers were sweeping through the city, massacring the native Christians and burning them alive in their homes. The first building to be burned was the chapel of the Methodist Mission in the Hatamen Street. Then flames sprang up in many quarters of the city. Amid the most deadening uproar, the Tung-tang or East Cathedral shot flames into the sky. The old Greek Church in the northeast of the city, the London Mission buildings, the handsome pile of the American Board Mission, and the entire foreign buildings belonging to the Imperial Marine Customs in the east city burned throughout the night. It was an appalling sight.

. . .On June 15th rescue parties were sent out by the American and Russian Legations in the morning, and by the British and German Legations in the afternoon, to save if possible native Christians from the burning ruins . . . Awful sights were witnessed. Women and children hacked to pieces, men trussed like fowls, with noses and ears cut off and eyes gouged out. Chinese Christians accompanied the reliefs and ran about in the labyrinth of network of streets that formed the quarter, calling upon the Christians to come out from their hiding places. All through the night the massacre had continued, and Boxers were even now caught red-handed at their bloody work. As their patrol was passing a Taoist Temple on the way, a noted Boxer meeting place, cries were heard within. The temple was forcibly entered. Native Christians were found there, their hands tied behind their backs, awaiting execution and torture, some had already been put to death, and their bodies were warm and bleeding. All were shockingly mutilated. Their fiendish murderers were at their incantations burning incense before their gods, offering Christians in sacrifice to their angered deities.[8]

In the event, 188 foreign missionaries and more than 32,000 Chinese believers lost their lives. This is not simply a story of cruelty and death, but also a testimony of God's people staying true to their Saviour despite desperate circumstances.

The reasons for the uprising of the Boxers were legion and had to do with the political defence of China and what is Chinese as much as with religious persecution. This is often part of the dynamic of persecution. Paul Cohen has analysed the reasons behind hatred of Christianity in China in his fascinating 'The Anti-Christian Tradition in China'.[9] With scholarly acumen, he argues that there was a strong tradition of hatred for Christianity and he charts the persecution of Christianity from as early as the 1600s in China, with opposition to and jealousy of the power of Adam

Schall (1591–1666), Jesuit astronomer to the court. The attacks ranged from the opposition of Confucianism to Christianity, to analyses of contradictions in Christianity, heterodoxy (heretical doctrine) and the imperialistic ambitions of Christianity. No doubt Catholic ideas about *imperium in imperio* – separate jurisdiction for Christian converts – were responsible for some of the hatred. One accusation was that some Chinese would convert to escape trial and this caused resentment of the missionaries, who were seen in a way as carrying out an imperial invasion inside Chinese territory. Later there were all kinds of slanders, ranging from those attacking the incoherence and inconsistencies of Christian thought to those even targeting the immorality of Christianity, with unpleasant and apparently wholly fabricated details as to its incestuous and homosexual practices.[10] Cohen finds that by the 1860s, 'vast sections of China seem literally to have been swamped with anti-Christian propaganda', as well as there being everything from a wall of indifference, a mountain of petty laws mitigating against conversion, countless stumbling blocks to missionary activity, and threats of terror expressed against anyone thinking of converting to the faith.[11]

All the while, the courage of the missionaries is evidenced by their writings. The goal of this book is to reflect on the courage of Christians in the face of extreme suffering. I have chosen therefore to mention some fascinating extracts from letters from missionaries during the Boxer holocaust. Along with the quotes at the head of this chapter, they make challenging reading.

Here Martin Linton, a young graduate of Oberlin Seminary in Taiku, writes to his sister:

February 15, 1900: Dear Anna . . . I confess, the enthusiasm I had when I left Oberlin Seminary at the end of summer has waned. The Lord's work is slow and tedious; we were happy to gain two new converts last year, for our presence here in rural Shanxi is not well regarded by most of the Chinese . . . Our medical station is a great service to the people here, with most of the patients being opium addicts . . . The drought makes people uneasy, and many Chinese blame the drought on us, saying that we have angered their gods by spreading our Christianity.

Many young boys have joined groups that call themselves The Boxers United in Righteousness. Do not fear; they pose no real threat to us because the Imperial government is fighting against them. Still, we have heard stories of them burning churches and attacking Chinese Christians, which does not endanger our lives as foreigners but makes our work of converting Chinese harder . . . We persevere in the faith, trusting that God will bless the Chinese who have come to know Him and will allow us to bring more into the fold. . .

June 10, 1900: We have heard that the Boxers have them surrounded and have destroyed the railroads and telegraph wires between the cities. Though we hear many accounts and predictions of Boxer violence, we cannot tell what is rumour and what is truth . . . My Chinese is now good enough that I could understand the chants of people outside the mission calling us 'white devils' . . . It is depressing, but it only strengthens our resolve and makes us yearn for the day when all of China will be brought into God's Holy Kingdom.

August 3, 1900: Though the Merciful Lord has spared our mission thus far, the political situation has changed . . . The Imperial Court has recognized the Boxers as part of the Ch'ing militia, and is at war with the US and European powers . . . On

July 31, the Imperial soldiers took the Oberlin mission in Taiku; the 6 foreign missionaries and at least 38 Chinese Christians there were all killed. Soldiers guard our mission now, so we cannot flee. I pray continuously that God will end the turmoil, but I know that His Divine Will is not for us to understand, so I pray that if our mission, and even our lives, should be lost in this struggle, that we will be judged to have been good and faithful servants.[12]

Taiyuan, the capital of Shansi Province in China, became the scene of one of the bloodiest massacres of modern-day Christianity. Also living in this capital city were a group of various missionaries dedicated to bringing the gospel to the Shansi region. Dr William Wilson operated a hospital for opium addicts at his own expense. He lived there with his wife and young son. Although he was already due for furlough, he had put it off because of the many victims of the famine that was ravaging the area. While he worked tirelessly on, he came down with peritonitis. Just after the killings started, Wilson travelled 20 miles to help a Chinese doctor who had been slashed by a Boxer sword. Although very sick, Wilson made the trip and was able to help the wounded man. On the way there, he penned his last letter. 'It's all fog,' he wrote to a fellow doctor, 'but I think, old chap, that we are on the edge of a volcano, and I fear Taiyuan is the inner edge.' He would not live to know how true those words were.

With Mrs Wilson were two China Inland Mission workers who were single. Jane Stevens, a nurse who was in frail health at the time, had arrived in China 15 years earlier, in 1885. During her last trip to England there were those who attempted to persuade her to stay in England. She replied,

'I don't feel I have yet finished the work God has for me in China. I must go back. Perhaps – who knows – I may be among those allowed to give their lives for the people.' Mildred Clarke, her fellow CIM missionary, wrote, 'I long to live a poured-out life unto Him among these Chinese, and to enter into the fellowship of His sufferings for souls, who poured out His life unto death for us.'

John and Sarah Young had been married only 15 months. They had made exceptional progress in Chinese, but were surrounded by uncertainty. 'I want to be found in the battle when He comes, and I want to be an instrument in the hands of God in saving souls from death.' So Sarah had written in application to join CIM. Eleven days before her death, she wrote, 'The winds may blow, the waves may roll high: If we keep our eyes off them and on the Lord, we shall be alright.'

Scottish evangelist Duncan Kay's wife managed to get a last letter off to her three children: 'I am writing this as it may be our last to you. Who knows but that we may be with Jesus very soon. This is only a wee note to send our dear love to you all, and to ask you not to feel sad when you know we have been killed. We have committed you all into God's hands. He will make a way for you all. Try to be good children. Love God. Give your hearts to Jesus. This is your dear parents' last request. Your loving Papa and Mama and wee Jenny.[13]

These are poignant testimonies to the mood of sacrifice and courage that prevailed among the missionary community at the turn of the century. 'Perhaps – who knows – I may be among those allowed to give their lives for the people,' writes one. Another writes, 'I long to live a poured-out life unto Him. . .' A mother writes, 'Try to be good children. Love God. Give your hearts to Jesus. This is your dear parents' last request.'

When the Boxer rebellion was spent in its venom, an assessment showed that the Chinese church had been battered but had never bent. Careful burials took place, and interest increased in Christianity because of the example of the martyrs and the continuation of the cause of Christ. Powerful soul-cleansing revivals swept across north China as Christians got right with God and a sense of conviction hung over the churches. In 1901 one missionary in Kiangsi Province reported 20,000 converts.

As favour briefly came back to the missionaries, it was a well-known fact that Christians had not demanded compensation for loss of property in the riots. Hudson Taylor, founder of the China Inland Mission, made the following call to those bringing the love of Christ to China: they were to show 'the meekness and gentleness of Christ, not only not to enter any claim against the Chinese government, but also to refrain from accepting compensation if offered'.

It is good to pause in this analysis to remember the passion that shaped a nation of that father of much Chinese Christianity, J. Hudson Taylor. Hudson Taylor coined the phrases 'If Jesus is not Lord of all He is not Lord at all', and 'God's work in God's time will always have God's provision'.

Hudson Taylor was born in Yorkshire, England, in 1832. After a brief period of teenage scepticism, he came to Christ by reading a Christian tract in his father's shop. A few months after his conversion, he consecrated himself wholly to the Lord's work. He sensed God was calling him to China, and he began studying medicine and lived on as little as possible, trusting God for his every provision.

In 1853, the 21-year-old Taylor sailed for China as an agent of a new mission society. He arrived in Shanghai the next spring and immediately began learning Chinese. Funds from home rarely arrived, but Taylor was determined to rely upon God for his every need, and he never appealed for money to his friends in England. Repeatedly he later told others, 'Depend upon it. God's work, done in God's way, will never lack for supplies.'

In those days, foreigners were not allowed into China's interior, and they were only allowed in five Chinese ports. Hudson Taylor, however, was burdened for those Chinese millions who had never heard of Christ. Ignoring the political restrictions, he travelled along the inland canals preaching the gospel.

In one of his early letters home he wrote:

> At home, you can never know what it is to be absolutely alone, amidst thousands, everyone looking on you with curiosity, with contempt, with suspicion, or with dislike. Thus to learn what it is to be despised and rejected of men . . . and then to have the love of Jesus applied to your heart by the Holy Spirit . . . this is precious, this is worth coming for.

By 1860, foreigners were able legally to travel anywhere in China, missionaries were allowed, and the Chinese were permitted to convert to Christianity. At a time when tremendous opportunities were opening up in China, ill health forced Taylor, with his wife and small daughter, to return to England. What seemed at first to be a setback in his mission work turned out to be a step forward. While in

England recovering his health, Taylor was able to complete his medical studies. He revised a Chinese New Testament and organised the China Inland Mission. The Mission's goal was this: to bring the gospel where it had never been brought before. Twenty-two people accompanied Taylor back to China in 1866. They were aware of the 'utter weakness in ourselves, we should be overwhelmed at the immensity of the work before us, were it not that our very insufficiency gives us a special claim to the fulfilment of His promise, "My grace is sufficient for thee; My strength is made perfect in weakness."'

It is worth noting that Hudson Taylor suffered to fulfil his calling: his daughter died from water on the brain; the family was almost killed in the Yang Chow riot of 1868; Maria, Taylor's first wife, died in childbirth; his second wife died of cancer; sickness and ill health were frequent. Yet the China Inland Mission continued its work of reaching China's millions for Christ. By 1895 the Mission had 641 missionaries plus 462 Chinese helpers at 260 stations. Under Hudson Taylor's leadership, CIM had supplied over half of the Protestant missionary force in China. During the Boxer rebellion of 1900, 56 of these missionaries were martyred and hundreds of Chinese Christians were killed.[14] The missionary work did not weaken, however, and the number of missionaries quadrupled in the coming decades.

Hudson Taylor wrote home to his friend, 'It was no vain or unintelligent act when, knowing this land, its people and climate, I laid my wife and children with myself on the altar for his service. And He who so unworthily we have been seeking to serve. . .He has not left us now.'

To his mother, he wrote more personally of his feelings at

the loss of his daughter, in a passage that shows the sufferings that these men and women were prepared to endure as they followed Christ:

> Our dear little Gracie! How we miss her sweet voice in the morning, one of the first sounds to greet us when we woke, and through the day and at eventide! As I take the walks I used to take with her tripping figure at my side, the thought comes anew like a throb of agony, 'Is it possible that I shall nevermore feel the pressure of that little hand. . . nevermore see the sparkle of those bright eyes?' And yet she is not lost. I would not have her back again. I am thankful she was taken, rather than any of the others, though she was the sunshine of our lives. I think I never saw anything so perfect, so beautiful as the remains of that dear child. The long, silken eyelashes under the finely arched brows; the nose so delicately chiselled; the mouth, small and sweetly expressive. . .Then her sweet little Chinese jacket, and the little hands folded on her bosom, holding a single flower – oh, it was passing fair.
>
> Pray for us. At times I seem almost overwhelmed with the internal and external trials connected with our work. But He has said: I will never leave thee or forsake thee, and 'My strength is made perfect in weakness'. So be it.[15]

### Seed that bears fruit: the story of Brother Yun

It is interesting to track the effect of the martyrdoms of the Boxer years. In his bestselling autobiography *The Heavenly Man*, Brother Yun charts the arrival of missionaries in the wake of the Boxer martyrdoms as the key to his finding faith, as the following extract from his account shows:

In September 1901, a large ship docked in Shanghai Port. A young single lady from Norway walked off the gangplank onto Chinese soil. Marie Monsen was one of a new wave of missionaries who, inspired by the martyrdoms of the previous year, had dedicated themselves to full-time missionary service in China. Monson stayed in China for more than thirty years. For a time she lived in my county where she encouraged and trained a small group of Chinese believers. . .

She didn't seem too concerned with making a good impression on the Chinese church leaders. She often told them, 'You are all hypocrites! You confess Jesus Christ with your lips while your hearts are not fully committed to Him! Repent before it is too late to escape God's judgment!' Hearts were convicted of sin and fires of revival swept throughout the villages of central China wherever she went.

So begins the recollection of Brother Yun and his remarkable tale of suffering and overcoming. I dwell on it here as just one of countless current stories of martyrs/witnesses in China and from China to the world today. They have lit a beacon which is burning in a dark world today. They have shown us afresh that the consecration of the apostles is a contemporary call to the Church worldwide. They call on us, in the words of Jim Elliot, to 'be ignitable'.

The heat of persecution in China was soon to be turned up again. China became a Communist nation in 1949. Within a few years all missionaries were expelled, church buildings were closed and thousands of Chinese pastors were imprisoned. Many lost their lives. Yun tells how his mother saw the missionaries leave Nanyang in the early 1950s, and how she never forgot the tears in their eyes as they headed for the coast under armed guard. Following this, Yun comments that in just one city in China, 49 Chinese pastors were sent to prison labour camps near the Russian border. Of these, 48 died in prison. When it came to his home area of Nanyang, believers were crucified on the walls of their churches for not denying Christ. One pastor was bound and attached to a long rope. The authorities, enraged that the man of God would not deny his faith, used a makeshift crane to lift him high into the air. Before hundreds of witnesses who had come to accuse him solely of being a 'counter-revolutionary', the pastor was asked one last time if he would recant. He shouted back, 'No! I will never deny the Lord who saved me!' The rope was released and the pastor crashed to the ground below.[16]

Yun is a remarkable man with a remarkable story. In my opinion, just to meet him is to meet the love of Jesus. Having become a Christian at the age of around 16, he became an effective, courageous preacher before being arrested and taken by the security police in December 1983. Here is how he got his nickname of the 'Heavenly Man'. The authorities were forcing him to lead them to where the underground church was hiding. 'What is your name? Where are you from? How many workers do you have? Where are they?' He alerted the church members to run by responding to his interrogators on the way: 'I'm a Heavenly Man. I live in gospel village! People call me Morning Star! My father's name is Abundant Blessing! My mother's name is Faith, Hope, Love!' Feigning madness in the manner of David in front of Abimelech, Yun was able to let his disciples escape.

Yun's infectious smile masks an experience of suffering for Christ that is in line with others in this book. On different occasions, he might have lost his life at the hands of his guards and torturers, which is why I include him in this book.

As the guards surrounded him on that day of arrest which was to lead to his near death, they kicked him with their steel-capped boots and struck him with their pistol handles. He testifies at that moment to hearing 'a gentle voice from above' that simply said two words to him: 'I know.' He was at that time reminded of the words of Christ to the persecuted believers in Smyrna: 'I know your afflictions and your poverty – yet you are rich! I know the slander of those who say they are Jews and are not, but are a synagogue of Satan. Do not be afraid of what you are about to suffer. I tell you, the devil will put some of you in prison to test you, and you will suffer persecution for ten days. Be faithful, even to the point of death, and I will give you the crown of life' (Rev. 2:9–10).

So begins a story of torture and suffering mingled, according to Yun, with intervention from heaven to give him physical strength to stand and continue to testify. This he does, remarkably throughout his times in prison, bringing some of the most dangerous characters to Christ, sometimes sharing or sacrificing his starvation food rations for others who oppose the gospel, that they might glimpse but a little of the love of Christ.

Here is some of his ordeal:

When the police van arrived at the Nanyang prison gate they took my handcuffs off the steel rail and pushed me out of the back of the van onto the frozen ground. A bitterly cold blizzard was blowing from the north. My face and hair were drenched with blood. My eyes were blackened and my face swollen. I had no shoes on my feet and the handcuffs had cut deeply into my wrists.

They took me into a large interrogation room. The man second in charge of the PSB arrogantly boasted, 'Yun, you have lost the fight today. Your co-workers are already in our hands . . . Your church is totally finished. You have completely failed. You are an enemy of our country and an enemy of the Party.' A spirit of faith spoke from within me, 'The gospel grows through hardship and will spread throughout the world . . . Truth is always truth. Nothing and no one can change that. It will always conquer.'

The officers stared at me with total disdain. One man, with a sinister smile, leaned forward and whispered, 'Yun, haven't you experienced enough suffering yet? Do you want us to "entertain" you some more? The policy of our government is to treat you well if you confess your crimes openly and honestly. But if you lie and don't cooperate we'll treat you harshly!' Another officer approached me with an electric baton. He turned the voltage up to the highest level and struck my face, head and various parts of my body with it. Immediately my body was filled with overwhelming agony, as if a thousand arrows had pierced my heart. The Holy Spirit encouraged me with Scriptures from the Bible: '*He was oppressed and He was afflicted, yet He opened not His mouth.*'

By meditating on the Word of God, the Lord strengthened me to endure. I realized any suffering I was to go through was nothing compared to what Jesus has suffered for me . . . Thank God He protected and preserved me through these trials. I knew that God was using the wrath of evil men to accomplish His purposes in me, to break down my self-centeredness and my stubbornness. I was a pitiful and dreadful sight. Like the Apostle Paul said, '*We have been made a spectacle to the whole universe, to angels as well as to men . . . Up to this moment we have become the scum of the earth, the refuse of the world.' 1 Corinthians 4:9, 13.*

The guards . . . forced me to crawl like a dog through the human faeces. They kicked me with their steel-capped boots, forcing me to roll over into the excrement. They even used their electric batons to stab me inside my mouth. I cannot easily describe the pain this caused. I thought my brain was going to explode.[17]

Through all this, Yun nearly lost his life. There was a time when his mother and sister were convinced that it was the end. His admirable, long-suffering wife Deling tells the story of one of their visits. Having been told to wait in a room, eventually a tiny figure was brought in, unconscious because he had been tortured just before their arrival. 'He looked like a little child, his ears shrivelled to the size of raisins.' So changed was he that at first they cried out to the authorities that they had brought the wrong man. Only when his mother saw his birthmark did she believe it was him. 'He was so little that he did not even look like a human being. His whole body was covered with bruises, torture marks, dried blood and dirt. Most of his hair had been torn out. . .' Then it was that he whispered to them not to despair, not to weep for him but to 'weep for the souls of men'. Yun told them he was going to be reunited with the Lord and so they should take the Lord's Supper for the last time before he died. After a time of communion and comfort they left, only to regroup in tears on the pavement outside the prison. Deling takes up the story:

We sat down outside the prison and cried out to the Lord: 'Father God of justice and mercy, please forgive our nation.

Have pity on those who persecute your children. . .' Many people were passing by when they heard us wailing. A crowd gathered and demanded to know what the matter was. Many wept as we told them what we'd seen that day.[18]

But he did not die. The rest of his imprisonment reads like pages from the book of Acts. As with Paul, the priority did not seem to be to get out of jail. It is interesting that there was no campaign to release him, at least not from Yun himself. Instead, like the apostle before him he concentrated his efforts on being an evangelist to the prisoners and to their guards. And wonders and signs of conversions ensued.

Listening to Yun today, watching his smile, seeing his tireless travelling and serving and loving communication of his deep burden, I believe Yun and others like him teach the Church in the West one thing and that is absolute consecration. Here is a man who is set apart. Here is a man who has died. As D.L. Moody said of his secret, 'There was a day when I died.' St Francis, talking about his conversion to Christ and to the poor, said, 'Not long after that, I left the world.' Of course this is the secret of the martyrs: they are not focusing on temporal crowns, nor on comfort. 'Paul was faithful, yet he ended up in prison. John the Baptist was faithful, yet he was beheaded. Millions of faithful people have been martyred, have lost everything, or have come to the end of life with nothing to show for it. *But the end of life is not the end.*'[19] They focus, as does the Chinese church with its world-shaping sacrifice, on eternity.

In late 2003, two events took place that seem to signal a shift in how China's house church movement sees itself. First, David Aikman's book *Jesus in Beijing* was published.[20]

Then China Soul for Christ Foundation issued Yuan Zhiming's DVD series *The Cross: Jesus in China*. Both of these journalistic works put names and faces on the house church movement. Previously, a veil of secrecy covered it. *Jesus in Beijing* introduces Western readers to house church leaders, based on interviews and research in China by the former Beijing bureau chief for *Time* magazine. *The Cross* is a powerful collection of interviews and testimonies, taped on location in China, of Christians from all walks of life, collected across three years. Yuan combines his talents as a filmmaker, philosopher and apologist as he weaves the dozens of stories together. Here we meet those arrested in the wake of the Cultural Revolution. Men like Moses Xe, testifying to God's word to him after 12 years in prison: 'Dear Child, My grace is sufficient to you.' His story of 23 years in prison without a Bible to start with, but with the song 'The Old Rugged Cross' to sustain him, leaves the watching world speechless. He tells the story of an important interrogation at the beginning where he could have lost his life had he replied without wisdom. The question fired at him was, 'You talk of heaven: Will Chairman Mao go to heaven?' Xe knew that if he said 'No' he would be beaten to death instantly, but having prayed a lot, he was able to reply, 'The door to heaven is WIDE open. Anyone can go to heaven if he acknowledges Jesus is the Son of God and repents of his sin: I am anxious for you all to believe. . .' Thus the interrogation, reminiscent of Paul before Festus and Agrippa in the book of Acts, continued.

Chinese Christians talk of the Bible being so rare that it became an invaluable treasure, with copies being made by hand and soaked with tears having been kissed by countless people. We meet also courageous Samuel Lamb, released from prison in 1978 having spent years in a cell only seven metres square. His testimony? 'Didn't my Lord tell me to take up my cross? The way of the cross surpasses all human understanding . . . The way of the cross is the way to sacrifice and victory.' Lamb tells movingly how 'jail has become the helpful training centre for the Church in China'.

These two works give us pictures, video testimonies and careful descriptions of house church ministries – and the house church leaders participated, apparently regardless of the risk of imprisonment inside China. Since then there has been some criticism of *Jesus in Beijing* and *The Cross* for putting Christians at risk of arrest. Following the release of these works, there seemed to be another time of persecution, with three prominent leaders being arrested in February 2004. But it is still not fully clear whether these materials played a role. Buildings used for church gatherings were razed to the ground. Careful analysis may yet show that the current wave of persecution started before the release of the works. Their willingness to talk to journalists and record their stories on video indicates that house church Christians, now numbering between 20 million and 70 million, are eager to preserve and to make public the marvellous story of the movement.

Time will tell whether China will become a Christian nation. The suffering continues. The governing edifice appears unshaken and prosperity is coming to China. And yet, the Chinese church, born out of the seed of martyrs dying and living, continues to grow and expand and spread out. The passion that shapes nations is at work in China.

# 12

# *Church of Martyrs – Islamic Persecution*

*'The public execution is to be understood not only as a judicial, but also as a political ritual. It belongs, even in minor cases, to the ceremonies by which power is manifested.'*
Michel Foucauld[1]

*'Among Religions, Christianity and Buddhism are primarily personal religions with mystical doctrines of love and contemplation. Mohamedanism and Bolshevism are practical, social, unspiritual, concerned to win the empire of this world.'*
Bertrand Russell[2]

One of the remarkable paradoxes of modern history is that the attacks of 9/11 by Islamic terrorists upon America and the West should have as their outcome the protection and advance of Islam in the very countries which radical Muslims attacked. Thus in Europe, the move to pass new laws against the incitement of religious hatred effectively may outlaw any careful critique of Islam as well as achieving its aim of curbing the expression of hatred. *The Times* reported, 'The Government believes the new "religious hatred offence" will . . . reassure Muslim

communities that have felt vulnerable since the 9/11 terrorist attacks.'[3] Another paradox is that no such equivalent
law to protect Christians will ever reach the statute books in
the current regimes of the Muslim world.

In that two-volume 'encyclopaedia of martyrs' published
under the unlikely title *Jesus Freaks*, Islam is cited as the
third most prolific cause of martyrdom of Christians in history, behind 'State Ruling Powers' and 'Atheism'. Whether,
as the twenty-first century dawns, that ranking will change
is an open question. It is certainly true that from Africa
through the Middle East through Pakistan across to Indonesia the number of Christian martyrs in Islamic states continues to rise sharply. The reason for this is that under
Islamic law one does not have the right to change one's religion. Muslims are happy to accept converts from other
religions, but a Muslim may not convert to another religion:
this remains, even in non-Muslim countries, an apostasy
punishable by death. Thus the thirteenth-century Islamic
commentator Bahdawi: 'Whosoever turns back from his
belief, openly or secretly, take him and kill him whereso-
ever you find him, like any other infidel. Separate yourself
from him altogether. Do not accept intercession in his
regard.'[4]

The book in which Bahdawi's comments are remembered, *Why I am not a Muslim*, is a careful, scholarly classic
after the manner of Bertrand Russell's *Why I am not a Christian*. First published in 1995, it is written by Ibn Warraq (a
pseudonym), a recovering Pakistani ex-zealot who was
originally shaken loose from his faith by the Salman
Rushdie affair.[5] Writing as a non-Christian, he is better
qualified than some to give some statistics on conversions

from Islam to Christianity (and therefore apostasy). These are hard to come by for obvious reasons. He cites evidence for 'thousands of Muslims abandoning Islam for Christianity from the middle ages to modern times, the most spectacular of these being, among others, Moroccan and Tunisian princes in the 17th century'. The Casa Dei Catecumeni has evidence of 1,087 conversions between 1614 and 1798. He affirms that after the massacres in Indonesia of the Communists in 1965, it is thought that as many as 2 to 3 million converted from Islam to Christianity, suffering bitter persecution ever since. In Europe, stories are beginning to emerge of persecution for those who convert and their need to go into hiding. In France alone some 200 to 300 people have converted from Islam to Christianity each year since the 1990s.[6] The persecution of Christians in 'tolerant' Egypt is well documented, with the number of deaths in the hundreds. Nevertheless, in Egypt conversions occur 'with enough frequency to anger Muslim clerics and mobilise public opinion behind proposals to enact a law to impose the death penalty for conversions'.[7]

Those who become Christians and stay in their Islamic country of origin do so at great risk. They routinely face arrest, confiscation of property, their marriage being declared null and void, their children being forcibly taken from them. Their family may take the law into their own hands and simply assassinate them.

This relentless pressure is the background to stories like that of 'Asif' told by, among others, Voice of the Martyrs.[8] Asif's story begins in Pakistan when, as a young, ambitious, worldly man, he has a motorcycle accident in which he suffers a broken foot. As he lies in the street in agony, a woman emerges from the crowd and prays to Jesus for his healing. Wondering how she dare do that for a Muslim, Asif is surprised that heat and power are coursing down his leg and that following the prayer he has no pain, the sickeningly awry foot is straightened and he is healed. Later receiving a Bible from the woman, Asif hungers to know more of Christ, asking the question, 'How can a man who is a mere prophet do this?' Reading the New Testament and learning of the miracles of Christ, he is drawn to and haunted by the question, 'Who is Jesus?' At the mosque he asks questions of the leaders. Their reaction is to question him as to what interest he could have in Jesus. Asif replies, 'How could I not have an interest? He healed me.' When the leaders realise the closeness of Asif to an experience of Christianity, he is locked up and then poisoned. Rather than allow him to convert, it is thought better for him to die while still a Muslim. During the night, lying in vomit and coming close to death as it seems, Asif cries to Christ for help and says to him that he wants to see him before he dies. Then one of those divine encounters of those under fire occurs. Asif testifies that the room in which he lay filled up with a bright light and his sickness diminished. Before him stood Jesus. It was at that moment that Asif surrendered the rest of his life to Christ, saying, 'God, this life is for you. As long as I am on earth I will work for you.'

Somehow managing to escape, Asif got home. His parents, on hearing about his encounter with Christ, told him that if he accepted Jesus he would have to leave home. So began Asif's life as a Christian. He felt he had no choice but to leave. He sought out the church, was discipled by a pastor and later baptised. From the beginning, he felt he had no choice but to speak about what Christ had done for him to all around him who would listen. Already as a very young Christian he knew trouble with the authorities and with the police. He was taken and beaten with heavy sticks and had his leg broken. His testimony is that as they beat him, he prayed that God would change their hearts and minds. He prayed for help and strength. His accusers continued and ordered him to leave the city. But he recovered slowly from his injuries and began preaching the gospel again. Taken at a meeting where he was speaking, the beatings began again with great severity. He comforts himself with Paul's perspective: 'For it has been granted to you on behalf of Christ not only to believe on him, but also to suffer for him' (Phil. 1:29). Asif continues to preach the gospel wherever he can in that hostile nation.[9]

Another story from Pakistan is one of an invisible and unnoticed courage. When I began to preach on these things, a member of our community in Oxford sent me a letter describing the story of Baker Perraiz, the 24-year-old son of a local pastor working as the school secretary of Murree Christian School in Pakistan. The school was attacked in 2002 by terrorists who were systematically targeting Christian and Western institutions. This is worthy of note but not, unfortunately, uncommon. Six people died. Four were guards and one was Baker. A maid told that she had been hiding in her employers' home when all the guns were firing. She heard Baker outside and told him to come in and hide with her, but he saw that one of the guards was lying on the ground, shot. She said, 'He could have saved himself, but he went off to help the guard. He was shot and died a few hours later. That was the sort of boy he was.' My friend added, 'I'm not exactly sure what constitutes a martyr, but I believe he died giving his life for a friend. In some ways Baker's was just a small act of love, probably not knowing the implications. But his life and sacrifice have made a tremendous impact on me for one, even though I was not there. I wonder if a lot of martyrs in the last years were not like Baker, little stories of courage that only a few people will know. I myself find it hard to think of martyrdom now as a glorious thing, but the lesson of Baker's life has been written on my heart.'

Muslims who come to faith even in almost-Christian countries are similarly at risk. I first met Abu Bakar when preaching at an Internationals Christmas party in Oxford. It was a great event with some 25 nationalities present, hosted by Commonwealth House, which has welcomed so many from all over the world over the years. Abu is tall, dark and passionate. He got my attention because as I wound up, he shouted at me not to stop preaching. I sat with him later and he told me his story of revelation and persecution. Abu was an imam of a Kampala mosque who had been brought up in a wealthy Ugandan Islamic family. He had frequently been on training trips, for example to Libya, where he said he had sat in meetings where the subject for the seminar had been 'Strategic steps to take for Britain to become an Islamic state'.

One day he had a vision in his prayer room. Writing on the wall was saying to him that he must be saved. Asking for help from his friends did not ease his troubled conscience. In the end another vision of Christ drove him into the chapel of Makere University. He slipped into a service, troubling those there as he was considered a threat to the

Christians. 'What is this disturber of Christians on campus doing here?' was the thought in students' minds. But when questioned, Abu said, 'I need to be saved, but I don't know what from. Please help me.'

The preacher that day 'just happened' to be Michael Kimule, close associate of John Mulinde. Both men are leaders of a remarkable work in Uganda which reaches even into government with its call to prayer and to the nation of Uganda to come back to Christ. These men were well suited to help Abu, who in time became a Christian and a disciple.

What followed this conversion was a wave of attacks on Abu's life. These came from his Islamic colleagues, and then from his close family. Such a visible convert to Christianity was evidently not to be countenanced. In the end his safety was at risk. I myself have seen the bullet marks in his leg that he received as he escaped for his very life. He moved as an official political refugee to England, where he is studying to be a lawyer and a preacher at one of the finest colleges in the land. His as yet unpublished paper 'The Uniqueness of Christ in Christianity and Islam' is a dangerous piece of dynamite for the cause of Christianity, as is his preaching. One could say of Abu (as was said of Latimer), 'Truly of Saul, God has created a Paul.' But I tell this everyday story of a chance meeting in Oxford to illustrate the constant risk that those who step into Christianity from Islam will suffer today.

Time fails me to mention many more individual cases in this cloud of courageous martyrs/witnesses who have suffered so bravely under Islamic skies. I will simply remember the courage of some in Iran, following the establishment of

Sharia law in the 1980s. The severest repression has come on Muslims who have become Christians. One of those was Hosein Soodman, an ordained Assemblies of God minister. Arrested in Gorgan, blindfolded, interrogated by police, he was forced to return to Mashad. There he was accused of spying, a charge which for his supporters was preposterous. 'He was a meek man who will be remembered for his quiet spirit.' He was there subjected to a public mockery for his faith and ordered to pray aloud repeatedly. His captors permitted his wife only two visits during his long imprisonment and denied her a final meeting before his hanging. When his wife heard his fate, she suffered a nervous breakdown. She and her four children, aged between ten and fifteen, were taken into the homes of Christians.

Another Iranian story is that of Anglican bishop Hassan Dehqani-Tafti, who was forced to leave Iran after the Islamic Revolution. His son Bahram Dehqani-Tafti was detained, bundled into a car and shot. Bishop Hassan remains convinced that his son died as a result of his Christian faith, and wrote the following prayer on the martyrdom of his son. It is a fitting tribute to the impossibility that persecution should extinguish the flame of the love of Christ.


O God
We remember not only our son but his murderers;
Not because they killed him in the prime of youth and made our
    tears flow,
Not because with this savage act they have brought further dis-
    grace on the name of our country
But because through their crime we now follow thy footsteps
    more closely in the way of sacrifice.

The terrible fire of this calamity burns up all the selfishness and
possessiveness in us;
Its flame reveals the depths of depravity and meanness and sus-
picion, the dimension of hatred and the measure of sinfulness
in human nature.
It makes obvious our need to trust in God's love as shown in the
cross of Jesus and his resurrection.

Love which makes us free from hate towards our persecutors;
Love which brings patience, courage, loyalty, humility, greatness
of heart;
Love which deepens our trust in God's final victory and his eternal designs;
Love which teaches us how to prepare ourselves to face our own
day of death.

O God
Our son's blood has multiplied the fruit of the spirit in the soil of
our souls;
When his murderers stand before thee on the day of judgement
Remember the fruit of the spirit by which they have enriched our
lives,
And forgive.[10]

Before we leave this all too brief look at these killing fields
of Christians, and the all too pervasive context for martyrdoms, there is another perspective that it is good to mention.

In April 2005, the *Spectator* magazine carried an article entitled 'Church of Martyrs' by Anthony Browne, Europe cor-
respondent of *The Times*. Browne charts how paradoxically
the war in 2003 in Iraq meant a new, unwelcome era for the
country's historic Christian community. When the war
stopped, persecution by Islamists, held in check by Saddam,

started. In Basra, the women of one church community complained of attacks against them for not wearing the Islamic veil. Browne saw many Christian-owned shops that had been firebombed. Two years and many church attacks later, Iraq may still be occupied by Christian foreign powers, but Browne found that the Islamists' plan to ethnically cleanse Iraq of its nearly 2,000-year-old Assyrian and Armenian Christian communities is reaching fruition.

He commented that rising nationalism and fundamentalism around the world has meant that Christianity is going back to its roots as the religion of the persecuted. There are now more than 300 million Christians who are either threatened with violence or legally discriminated against simply because of their faith – more than any other religion.

> Christians are no longer thrown to the lions. But from China, North Korea and Malaysia, through India, Pakistan and Sri Lanka to Egypt, Saudi Arabia and Turkey, they are subjected to legalised discrimination, violence, imprisonment, relocation and forced conversion. Even in supposedly Christian Europe, Christianity has become the most mocked religion, its followers treated with public suspicion and derision and sometimes – such as the would-be EU commissioner Rocco Buttiglione – hounded out of political office.[11]

In many parts of the Islamic world, Christians are systematically discriminated against and persecuted. Saudi Arabia – for Browne the 'global fountain of religious bigotry' – bans churches, public Christian worship, the Bible and the sale of Christmas cards, and stops non-Muslims from entering Mecca. In 1992 a Saudi national Christian, Abdul Kareem Mal-Allah, was beheaded for 'insulting' God by speaking negatively of the prophet Muhammad. Christians are regularly imprisoned and tortured on trumped-up charges of drinking, blaspheming or Bible-bashing, as some British citizens have found. In 2005, furthermore, Saudi Arabia announced that only Muslims can become citizens.

The Copts of Egypt make up half the Christians in the Middle East, the cradle of Christianity. They inhabited the land before the Islamic conquest, and still make up a fifth of the population. By law they are banned from being president of the Islamic Republic of Egypt and from attending Al Azhar University, and are severely restricted from joining the police and army. By practice they are banned from holding any high political or commercial position. Under the nineteenth-century Hamayouni decrees, Copts must get permission from the president to build or repair churches – but he usually refuses. Mosques face no such controls.

Browne continues his analysis, citing government-controlled television broadcasts of anti-Copt propaganda, while giving no airtime to Copts. Christian girls – and even the wives of Christian priests – are abducted and forcibly converted to Islam, recently prompting mass demonstrations. A report by Freedom House in Washington concludes, 'The cumulative effect of these threats creates an atmosphere of persecution and raises fears that during the 21st century the Copts may have a vastly diminished presence in their homelands.'

In the world's most economically successful Muslim nation, Malaysia, the world's only deliberate affirmative action programme for a majority population ensures that Muslims are given better access to jobs, housing and education. In the world's most populous Muslim nation, Indonesia, some 10,000 Christians have been killed in the last few years by Muslims trying to Islamicise the Moluccas.

In the Islamic Republic of Pakistan, most of the five million Christians live as an underclass, doing work such as toilet-cleaning. Under the Hudood ordinances, a Muslim can testify against a non-Muslim in court, but a non-Muslim cannot testify against a Muslim. Blasphemy laws are abused to persecute Christians. In the last few years, dozens of Christians have been killed in bomb and gun attacks on churches and Christian schools.

In Nigeria, 12 states have introduced Sharia law, which affects Christians as much as Muslims. Christian girls are forced to wear the Islamic veil at school, and Christians are banned from drinking alcohol. Thousands of Christians have been killed in the last few years in the ensuing violence.

Even in what was, before multiculturalism, known as Christendom, Christians are persecuted. Browne interviewed dozens of former Muslims who have converted to Christianity in Britain, and found them shunned by their community, subjected to mob violence, forced out of town, threatened with death and even kidnapped. The Barnabas Trust knows of 3,000 such Christians facing persecution in this country, but the police and government do nothing.

Dr Paul Marshall, senior fellow at the Centre for Religious Freedom in Washington, estimates that there are 200 million Christians who face violence because of their faith, and 350 million who face legally sanctioned discrimination in terms of access to jobs and housing. The World Evangelical Alliance wrote in a report to the UN Human Rights Commission in 2004 that Christians are 'the largest single group in the world which is being denied human rights on the basis of their faith'.

Anthony Browne rounds up his analysis, writing as a non-Christian, with an important reflection: 'Part of the problem is old-style racism against non-whites; part of it is new-style guilt. If all this were happening to the world's Sikhs or Muslims simply because of their faith, you can be sure it would lead the 10 o'clock News and the front page of the *Guardian* on a regular basis. But the BBC, despite being mainly funded by Christians, is an organisation that promotes ridicule of the Bible, while banning criticism of the Qur'an.' Dr Paul Marshall said, 'Christians are seen as Europeans and Americans, which means you get a lack of sympathy which you would not get if they were Tibetan Buddhists.'

Christians themselves are partly to blame for all this. Christianity uniquely defines itself by its persecution, and its forgiveness of its persecutors. To this day, while Muslims stick up for their co-religionists, Christians – beyond a few charities – have given up such forms of discrimination. Dr Sookhdeo, leader of the Barnabus Trust, said, 'The Muslims have an Ummah [the worldwide Muslim community] whereas Christians do not have Christendom. There is no Christian country that says, "We are Christian and we will help Christians."' Browne concludes:

As a liberal democrat atheist, I believe all persecuted people should be helped equally, irrespective of their religion. But the guilt-ridden West is ignoring people because of their religion. If non-Christians like me can sense the nonsense, how does it make Christians feel? And how are they going to react?

My answer would be: with courage! Christians in the face of this are called to passionate, courageous, tenacious holding on to Christ. They are still called to 'go into all the world and make disciples', however difficult this may seem. They are called to a heavenly perspective in the face of suffering, which knows that this life is not the only life. This will also persuade and convince others, as it has done in the past, of the divinity and kindness of Christ. At the same time Christians are called to 'defend the cause of justice', and to 'defend the fatherless and the widow'. And this will include defending the persecuted Christian minorities in this global village. It will include championing their cause, visiting them in prison, speaking out in public and in the corridors of power and broadcasting, and shaking off some of the post-colonial guilt which makes the Church and her leaders dumb, or leads them in bizarre cases to defend the very people who are attacking her. This will take great courage and clarity, but the best is yet to be. This gospel will be preached to all nations, Jesus said, and no doubt a time is coming for more and more fruitful, courageous preaching in these 'impossible' areas.

Browne is hinting above that he fears a 'Christian fundamentalist backlash'. And Christians need also to beware of reacting with counter-persecution, even if such a thing were possible. Instead, as I have said, let there be a wave of love and friendship going out to Islamic neighbours, and let there be imitation of Christ in so far as we can discern what it is to follow in his footsteps today.

# 13

## For Such a Time as This

*'The Holy Ghost does not come on machinery, but on men.'*
E. M. Bounds[1]

The time of history we live in requires dedicated, transformed, consecrated men and women. What is required for such a time as this is the passion that shapes nations.

The Bible is full of references to time. The most important event of all history happened only when the time had fully come. Then it was that God sent forth his Son. At the start of his loving, world-changing work, Jesus spoke to his mother about his time not being yet come. He would not go up to the feast because, as he said: 'My time is not yet.' He says, 'I'm only with you a short time and then I'm going to my Father.' But in the end he does go to the feast, and it is as if his kingdom is by then unstoppable. Finally, he pronounces, at the last supper: 'Father, the time has come: Glorify your Son. . .'

In passages which, in the light of current climatic and terrorist events, have a haunting ring, Jesus said: 'You know how to interpret the appearance of the sky, but you cannot interpret the signs of the times' (Matt. 16:3). In enigmatic terms, he says: 'Jerusalem will be trampled on by the Gentiles until the times of the Gentiles are fulfilled. Men will faint from terror. . .' (Luke 21:24, 26).

Among many Old Testament references, it was said that the 'men of Issachar . . . understood the times and knew what Israel should do' (1 Chron. 12:32). Ecclesiastes says the 'wise heart will know the proper time' (Ecc. 8:5). Hosea calls us to 'break up your unploughed ground; for it is time to seek the Lord' (Hosea 10:12).

But the incident which sticks to the thinking of this book so that it cannot be dislodged as a 'now word' for the Church, in my opinion, is the challenge made to Queen Esther: 'Who knows but that you have come into the kingdom for such a time as this?' I want to apply some lessons from this story to today.

The familiar story is that her uncle, Mordecai, discovers that the people of God will be destroyed. He calls on Esther to stand up and dare to go in to the king. Esther refuses, as she fears for her life. Mordecai utters the unforgettable statement of Esther 4:13–14:

> Do not think that because you are in the king's house you alone of all the Jews will escape. For if you remain silent at this time, relief and deliverance for the Jews will arise from another place, but you and your father's family will perish. And who knows but that you have come to royal position for such a time as this?

Esther's reaction was to call a fast, to pray for three days, to gather others, to get a strategy. And the situation is poised for the intervention of God.

## Time of danger

The story starts with the discovery of a plot of ethnic cleansing. It stands as a prophetic symbol for the people of God through the ages facing the one who comes to steal and kill and to destroy. In Revelation 12, the dragon stands before the woman about to give birth to devour him before he was born. He stood before Moses. He stood before the innocents at the time of the birth of Jesus. Who knows but that he stands roaring at the people of God today?

It is a time of danger, I believe, for our nations and for the people of God. In Britain, we see the powerless under siege: embryo research; abortion laws; assisted dying: an ethical shift that has pushed aside biblical values in favour of a postmodern value system where anything goes and where the ancient signposts have been pulled up with nothing to replace them. We live in a violent society where children are increasingly at risk, with the age of consent being lowered, and recent teenage murders at school, as well as stories of one in three being bullied and one in three children having carried an offensive weapon to school. There is a spirit of violence in the land. We see a drunken, violent, madly bingeing teenage and young adult culture. The reputation of England and America is in trouble, with stories of abuse of prisoners by our armies. We live in a culture of addiction, where sex is god, and Internet porn is becoming normal currency for movies and plays, as the country slides into scenes reminiscent of Rome before its fall. We are an addicted society.

As well as this, part of the background menace that children grow up with today is terror. In an all too prophetic text, Leviticus 26:14 says: 'But if you will not listen to me and carry out all these commands, and if you reject my decrees and abhor my laws . . . and so violate my covenant, then I will do this to you: I will bring upon you sudden terror.' It was in the wake of 9/11 that I began to collect headlines such as this: 'Allah is great and we will die killing' (shouted out by the Madrid bombers when under siege); 'I always say I want to see the Islamic flag over 10 Downing Street' (from the leader of El-Muhajiroun, a party dedicated to the overthrow of Western society)[2]. I realise this is a 'radical' view not representative of the vast majority of Muslims. Again I call not for a fearful reaction to the Islamic community, but one of friendship and care. But as far as 'radical Islam' is concerned, it is nevertheless a time of danger.

## Time of intimidation

But also in this story, it is a time of intimidation. Esther sees the danger, but she is intimidated into inaction. Even seeing the danger described above, many may be intimidated into silence for fear of prosecution under the terms of the new laws in Europe regarding 'incitement to religious hatred', even though no hatred is being peddled, but rather an incitement to loving prayer. What is being incited is that Christians get courage, and join in a tidal wave of love and friendship and communication of the love of God to the poor in spirit throughout the land.

But the Church is intimidated. Esther says that for any woman who approaches the king without being summoned, the king has but one law: to be put to death. She is intimidated into silence. And today in our nation the

Church is intimidated. One example is her difficulty as regards any reservations she may have about homosexuality. Incidentally, it is worth noting the complete turn around that has occurred in the space of 40 years. Back then, homosexuality was a crime for which you could go to prison. First there was a legalisation, then a lowering of the age of consent from 21 to 18; then a lowering from 18 to 16. And now it has almost become a crime for which one might go to prison to suggest that this practice may be wrong or 'against nature'. The Church which seeks to be beautifully inclusive and winsomely holy is under fire in the media as homophobic.

A parable of courage for the Church today is Jesus' treatment of the woman taken in adultery. A religious crowd wanted to stone her. Jesus refused. However, his inclusive love was not without holy calling to a new lifestyle. He looked into the eyes of the woman and said: 'Go and sin no more.' Somehow in the extraordinary gaze of Christ there was forgiveness for questions of sexual identity, and the hope of being able to go and sin no more. Yet instead of this radiant, counter-cultural body of Christ, the Church today, when faced with homosexuality, hardly dares to mention sin in this context. She is intimidated like Esther was into silence.

As regards the fame and the name of Christ, there is intimidation. In our land, martyrs have shed their blood for the honour of the efficacy of the passion of the Christ. Yet this is dragged shamelessly into derision. Recent showings of anti-Christian TV programmes would have been unthinkable even ten years ago. I have already cited Anthony Browne's judgement that the 'BBC is an organisation that promotes ridicule of the Bible, while banning criticism of the Qur'an'.

When Mel Gibson's film *The Passion of the Christ* was released, it caused a storm of invective. It is worth wondering why. Surely it was not the violence, as so many films are so very violent. Here is a typical review from Richard Eyre in *The Guardian*:

> I know I'm supposed to believe that Christ died for our sake, was crucified under Pontius Pilate, suffered death, was buried and on the third day rose again in accordance with the Scriptures, but does it all have to be so fatuously literal?

He continues in this scornful vein and concludes:

> *The Passion of the Christ* reflects an angry longing to return to a medieval world, uncomplicated by liberal ambiguity and scepticism. It's perfectly timed to coincide with the politics of the Bush administration. The plague of fundamentalism has remained dormant for centuries only to become virulent in the 21st century. Religion is being put back into religion.[3]

Nor was such intimidation confined to the Anglophone press. Under the headline 'La régression Gibson', *Le Monde* awarded this box office breaking movie the following verdict:

> With religious extremism gaining ground everywhere, this film could have a truly devastating effect. . .No surprise then that Gibson's support comes from the ranks of traditional Catholics for whom the guilt of the Jews for the death of Jesus is self-evident. This film is part of the worst fundamentalist tendencies of the modern world.[4]

Just for the record, I am one of many who believe that the film is a careful account, far from excessively violent, of what it has said it is: 'The Passion of the Christ'. Mel Gibson describes what he is trying to do in the following way: 'The film had its genesis in a period in which I found myself trapped with feelings of terrible isolated loneliness.'

His sources were the work of artists like Caravaggio, Mantegna, Masaccio, Pierro della Francesca, and above all the Bible. He continues:

> There is a classical Greek word which best defines what 'truth' guided my work: *alethia,* it simply means 'unforgetting'. From *lethe* – water from Homer's river Lethe caused forgetfulness. It has unfortunately become part of the ritual of our modern secular existence to forget. The film. . .does enumerate the facts described in Holy Scripture. It is not merely representative or expressive. I think of it as contemplative.[5]

It is interesting that this 'unforgetting' of this story has caused such scorn, and such intimidation. Because of such intimidation the Church can be silenced, like Esther.

## Time for courage

The burden of this book has been to say: When these intimidations occur, take heart, look up. The Church has been lulled into a false sense of security and assimilated with the culture, but in fact Jesus calls us to be radically, bravely, lovingly counter-cultural, whatever it takes. Such intimidation is only to be expected: Take courage!

I remember when Christian politician Ann Widdecombe visited our church for a Q and A with hundreds of students. She was asked whether she suffered or felt under threat for her position as a Christian. Her reply was salutary: 'St Paul was thrown to the lions, St Peter was crucified upside down and all I get is Jeremy Paxman. Let us not exaggerate.'

The book of Esther is a story of courage. Esther decides to risk her life. And in our nation it is a time for the courage of Esthers: young women who will take a risk. It is time for Daniels, for Gideons, for John the Baptists. It is time for Latimers and Tyndales and Hanningtons and Bonhoeffers. It is a time for the passion that changes nations.

The anatomy of courage implies a completely transformed life. Esther starts the story as insular, unconcerned, unaware and unprepared. She goes through a transformation to courage, concern, consecration and creative commitment. She gives up her life: 'And if I perish, I perish,' is her considered decision. Many of the martyrs/witnesses have reached the point that they have abandoned everything for the sake of Christ. They are Dead Men Walking (the Grateful Dead, if it is not an unhelpful image! Dead to the world and its ambitions and on fire with consuming affection for God). Time has failed me to tell of great men and women whose stories can set our hearts thumping. I have not been able to tell of those who advanced the kingdom of God into forbidden, impossible areas; transformed men like Jim Elliot and Nate Saint, martyred together by the Auca Indians in the 1950s. The life and death of Jim Elliot was a testimony of a man committed to the will of God. He sought God's will, pleaded for it, waited for it, and, most importantly, obeyed it.

His martyrdom at 28 and subsequent books on his life by his former wife, Elisabeth Elliot, have been the catalyst for sending thousands into the mission fields and stoking the fires of a heart for God. He was an intense Christian, bent on pleasing God alone and not man. '[He makes] His ministers a flame of fire,' Elliot wrote while a student at Wheaton College. 'Am I ignitable? God deliver me from the dread asbestos of "other things". Saturate me with the oil of the Spirit that I may be aflame. But flame is transient, often short-lived. Canst thou bear this my soul – short life? In me there dwells the spirit of the Great Short-Lived, whose zeal for God's house consumed Him.'

Elliot lost his life forcibly advancing the kingdom. Others in this book have died defending ground already taken, resisting and refusing to give up. Such were the Huguenots of France, who merit a whole book to themselves. When the semi-political fury of the St Bartholomew's Day massacre unfurled on an unsuspecting Protestant Church, on the 24th August 1572, 10,000 lost their lives in Paris alone, and the massacres were repeated throughout France[6]. In scenes prefiguring Hutu/Tutsi killings in Rwanda, few were noble enough to decline to become the executioners of their friends. Here we remember the exemplary courage and transformed life of Marie Durand, a true Esther. To this day can be seen the word 'résister' which she carved on her prison wall with her bare fingers during her 60-year imprisonment in the Tour de Constance.[7] Another is Antoine Court, who at the age of 20 returned to the Cévennes to gather the preachers together again into the first Synod in the Desert at the constant risk of his life. Each September in front of the Musée du Désert near Nimes, 10,000 Protestants gather to remember them. Inside this museum are the stirring memorials of those carted off to the galleys, separated from their families[8]. People like Migault who suffered the billeting upon them of the dreaded 'dragonnades', soldiers of Louis XIV, and who nevertheless refused to renounce their faith. His wife was nearly burned to death in her own home. But 'this good woman, knowing whom she believed, did not for a moment lose the composure of her mind. She cast all her cares and sufferings upon her saviour; repelled the repeated threats to change her religion with equal mildness and resolution, until swooning away she became insensible to further insult and injury.'[9]

This is perhaps the heart of the matter, for in the end, this book contains a challenge to get back the courage of the martyrs and with it their passionate and compassionate love for their persecutors and for those who still need to hear of Christ. E.M. Bounds once put it like this:

> Men are God's method. The Church is looking for better methods; God is looking for better men. What the Church needs today is not more machinery or better, not new organizations or more and novel methods, but men whom the Holy Ghost can use: men of prayer, men and women mighty in prayer. The Holy Ghost does not come on machinery, but on men. He does not anoint plans, but men – men of prayer.[10]

## Time for strategy

Esther says that for any woman who approaches the king without being summoned, the king has but one law: she must be put to death. The only exception to this is when the king extends the royal sceptre. This is not only a picture of intimidation but it is also a haunting picture of prayer. The intercessor is called to go in to the King of kings, risking death unless he extends his sceptre. This has been provided in Jesus, of whom Balaam prophesies: *'I see him, but not now; I behold him, but not near. A star will come out of Jacob; a sceptre will rise out of Israel* (Num. 24:17).

One call of this book is to come under the sceptre of the mercy of the cross to get into the presence of the King. We need to answer the worldwide call to become an intercessory people.

The story continues with strategy: Esther invites the people to fast (and by implication, pray) for three days and she says for her part she and her attendants will fast too. This shows her understanding that the destiny of nations is not in the hands of politicians but in the hands of the people of God who pray. In the Church in the West there is very little strategy. Perhaps it is that things are not yet desperate enough. I believe on the contrary that they are desperate. I believe we need a strategy in every department, but perhaps above all, like Esther, in the realm of prayer. In Oxford, we are pursuing a strategy that looks like this:

- Every Christian an Intercessor
- Every Home a Prayer Altar
- Every Church a House of Prayer
- Every Town an Inter-church Prayer Centre.

I believe the Church is under threat as in the days of Esther and she needs to awaken to a coherent strategy. Often it is the world that is awake and asking questions but the Church that sleeps.

Sometimes I liken England to a person from whom one evil spirit has been expelled, but whose final condition is worse than the first. This is an image that may also apply in these years to Iraq. In Saddam Hussein a devil was cast out of the country who held it in the grip of terror. But who is to say if his place has not been taken by seven spirits worse than the first? Time will tell.

Jesus said:

When an evil spirit comes out of a man, it goes through arid places seeking rest and does not find it. Then it says, 'I will return to the house I left.' When it arrives, it finds the house unoccupied, swept clean and put in order. Then it goes and takes with it seven other spirits more wicked than itself, and they go in and live there. And the final condition of that man is worse than the first. That is how it will be with this wicked generation. (Matt. 12:43–45)

England received the Bible early. Our constitution was written with an open Bible beside it. Men gave their blood to bring us the gospel in our own language. And yet the swept-clean land has been, it seems, invaded by darkness. Its final condition is worse than its first. If Jesus said of a boy his disciples could not cleanse, 'This kind comes out only through prayer with fasting,' it is reasonable to suppose that the unbelieving, unclean, violent, even anti-Christian spirit that we see at work will only come out by prayer with fasting: hence the above strategy!

**Time for God**

In this chapter I have said that we live in a time of danger, a time of intimidation, a time for courage, a time for prayer and strategy and transformation. But the story of Esther ends with. . .God. And this is the hopeful message. It is that with God all things are possible. And for our countries under siege, a complete turning back to God is possible. We are looking for it, but it will take courage. For Esther, what happens is so subtle and fascinating: she invites the king to a feast and he asks her what she desires. But she holds back, and instead invites him to a second feast the following day. Why does she do this? Presumably because it is not yet the time for God.

And then, beautifully, the miracles begin to occur. God is at work. Fasting and prayer are heard in heaven. So it is that during the night the second day after the fast, something happens. Something 'out of the box'. Something from God. The king cannot sleep. He remembers the loyalty of Mordecai, and he honours him. And the rescue of the Jews is beginning. The following day, Esther has the ear of the king, who grants her a revocation of the edict against her: a change in the law of the land, protection for the people of God.

And this is our hope today: a hope for the intervention of God. And in our nation, we're looking for something. . . looking to God: like Simeon waiting for the consolation of Israel, like Anna looking for the redemption of Jerusalem. Luther King cried out, 'I have a dream.' John Knox called out, 'Give me Scotland or I die.' Where are the imitators of Christ who will have a dream and who will risk their lives? Where are those who will be the martyrs/witnesses calling out in the wilderness: 'Give me England or I die'? Where is the brave Church which loves not its life so much as to shrink from death? My prayer is that this short book of unforgetting will help call her into being.

# Notes

## Chapter 1: The Martyrs' Memorial

1. Mark Stibbe, *Fire and Blood: The Work of the Spirit; The Work of the Cross* (Monarch, 2001), p. 59.

2. For more, see www.viva.org.

3. For more, see www.arocha.org.

4. Heb. 11:32.

5. John 21:25.

## Chapter 2: Martyrdom or Suicide?

1. Robert Southwell, 'An Epistle of Comfort' 1587, in Brad Gregory, *Salvation at Stake* (Harvard University Press, 1999), p. 315.

2. Jasper Ridley, *Bloody Mary's Martyrs: The Story of England's Terror* (Constable and Robinson, 2001), p. 117.

3. Brother Andrew's message at St Aldate's, Oxford, October 2004.

4. Ibid.

## Chapter 3: Paul and Peter

1. Karl Barth, in Robertson, *Paul Schneider* (SCM, 1956) p. 125.

2. Around AD 64, as Clement, Dionysius and Eusebius all concur (Stevenson, *A New Eusebius* [SPCK, 1963] pp. 4, 5).

3. Ibid.

4. See Jules Thobois, *Le Regard Extraordinaire* (Editions Vida, 1992).

5. 'We are witnesses. . .' (Acts 10:38). See also Luke 24:48; Acts 1:8; 5:32; 10:41.

6. W.H.C. Frend, *The Rise of Christianity* (DLT, 1984), p. 110.

7. First published in 1563 under the title 'Actes and Monuments of These Latter Perilous Dayes Touching Matters of the Church'. The quotations in this book are from the Hendrickson Christian Classics Edition 2004.

8. Brother Yun and Paul Hattaway, *The Heavenly Man* (Monarch Publications, 2002), p. 80. Used by permission.

### Chapter 4: Polycarp and Chrysostom

1. Dietrich Bonhoeffer, *The Cost of Discipleship* (SCM, 2001), p. 81.

2. *c.* AD 212, in Stevenson, *A New Eusebius*, p. 169.

3. Ibid., p. 169.

4. Ibid., p. 230.

5. *A New Eusebius*, op. cit., pp.19–24.

6. Frend, *The Rise of Christianity*, p. 182.

7. Stevenson, *A New Eusebius*, p. 35.

8. Edward Gibbon, *Decline and Fall of the Roman Empire* (Modern Library, 2005), p.550.

9. Ed. Philip Schaff, *Ante and Post Nicene Fathers*, vol. 9, pp. 14–15.

### Chapter 5: Wycliffe and Tyndale

1. *Foxe's Book of Martyrs*, ch. 7.

2. In Brian Moynahan, *William Tyndale* (Abacus, 2003), p. 104.

3. Ibid., p. 116.

4. *Foxe's Book of Martyrs*, pp. 225ff.

5. See Esther 4:14, 'Who knows but that you have come to royal position for such a time as this?'

6. Probably William Latimer, a friend of Erasmus, under whom Tyndale had studied at Oxford. See Moynahan, *William Tyndale*, p. 405.

7. Ibid., p. 32.

8. Ibid., p. 195.

9. The Yale edition of More's complete works contains his attacks on Tyndale and his fellow evangelicals. See Moynahan, ibid., pp. 395ff.

10. Ibid., p. 290.

11. *Foxe's Book of Martyrs*, op. cit., pp. 232–3.

### Chapter 6: Latimer and Ridley

1. Michel Foucauld, *Discipline and Punish* (original title *Surveiller et Punir*) (Penguin, 1991), p. 49.

2. Quotes on Latimer are from *The Columbia Encyclopedia*, Sixth Edition (Columbia University Press, 2001).

3. Merle d'Aubigne, *The Reformation in England* (Banner of Truth, 1977), p. 207.

4. Quotations from 'Sermon on the Plough' are from *Selected Writings* by Hugh Latimer, Ed. Arthur Pollard (Fyfield Books, 2000).

5. Ridley, *Bloody Mary's Martyrs*, p. 114.

6. *Foxe's Book of Martyrs*, p. 301.

### Chapter 7: Archbishop Thomas Cranmer

1. Pierre Brully's final letter to his wife, 18th February 1546, in Gregory, *Salvation at Stake*.

2. In Gordon Rupp, *Six Makers of English Religion* (Hodder and Stoughton, 1957), p. 37.

3. The famous line, 'Who will rid me of this turbulent priest?' was spoken by Henry II about Thomas à Becket and led to his death.

4. Thomas More amazed his friends by his courage. He who had pursued and prosecuted Tyndale with such ferocity was himself arrested for refusing to condone Henry's divorce or sign the Act of Supremacy. At the scaffold, he assured the crowd that he died 'the king's good servant, but God's first'. He even comforted his executioner: 'Today you will do me a greater favour than any other mortal man is able to do to me; pluck up your spirit man and don't be afraid to do your duty.' In D.C. Talk, *Jesus Freaks II* (Bethany House, 2002), p. 255.

5. *Foxe's Book of Martyrs*, op. cit., p. 692.

6. Diarmaid MacCulloch, *Thomas Cranmer* (Yale University Press, 1996), p. 360.

7. Ibid., p. 381.

8. Ibid., p. 382.

9. Ibid., p. 567.

10. Ridley, *Bloody Mary's Martyrs*, pp. 125–138.

11. For a good summary of the event, see Jan Morris, *The Oxford Book of Oxford* (OUP, 1978), p. 47.

12. See MacCulloch, *Thomas Cranmer*, p. 603, for this version.

## Chapter 8: Edmund Campion

1. Moynahan, *William Tyndale*, p. 116.

2. This at least is the view of *The Catholic Encyclopaedia*.

3. 'It is a great pity to see so notable a man leave his country, for indeed he was one of the diamonds of England' (Cecil to Hanihurst, in Evelyn Waugh, *Edmund Campion* [OUP, 1935], p. 57).

4. Ibid., p. 62.

5. Ibid., p. 61.

6. *Catholic Online Encyclopedia*: Edmund Campion. See www.newadvent.org

7. Ibid.

8. 'Campion's Brag', quoted in full as an appendix to Waugh, *Edmund Campion*.

## Chapter 9: James Hannington and the Uganda Martyrs

1. Andrew Chandler, *The Terrible Alternative: Christian Martyrdom in the 20th Century* (Continuum, 1998), p. 12.

2. For more on this, see chapter 15 of Ibn Warraq, *Why I am not a Muslim* (Prometheus, 2003).

3. For this account see www.buganda.com/martyrs.htm

4. Sandy Millar's sermon on 'Homosexuality and the stand of the African churches', quoted in *UK Focus*, autumn 2003.

## Chapter 10: Dietrich Bonhoeffer and Paul Schneider

1. Martin Luther King, assassinated in Memphis, Tennessee, 1968, in *Jesus Freaks II*.

2. Robertson, *Paul Schneider – Pastor of Buchenwald* (SCM, 1956), p. 63.

3. Bishop Bell of Chichester's foreword to Dietrich Bonhoeffer, *The Cost of Discipleship* (SCM, 1959), p. 7.

4. Leibholz's 'memoir', ibid., p. 9.

5. In D. C. Talk, *Jesus Freaks* (Eagle, 2000), p. 198.

6. Bonhoeffer, *The Cost of Discipleship*, p. 81.

7. Michael F. Moeller, 'Remembering Dietrich Bonhoeffer' in *International Encyclopedia of Philosophy*.

8. Ibid., p. 15.

9. In Rupp, *Six Makers of English Religion*.

10. So begins Robertson's translation of his widow's biography, *Paul Schneider*.

11. Ibid., p. 41.

12. Ibid., p. 56.

13. Ibid., p. 63.

14. Ibid., p. 114.

15. Ibid., p. 125.

## Chapter 11: Chinese Christianity – Crucified with Christ

1. In James and Marti Hefley, *By Their Blood: Christian Martyrs from the Twentieth Century and Beyond* (Baker Books, 1979), p. 19.

2. In Yuan Zhiming, *The Cross: Jesus in China*, DVD (China Soul for Christ Foundation, 2003).

3. Hefley, *By Their Blood*, p. 16.

4. 'Had our commercial relationship been free of blame it is still most probable that China would have put obstacles in the way of national intercourse. How much more so when, under the English flag, unprincipled men commenced to smuggle opium into the country' (Broomhall, ed., *The Martyred Missionaries of the China Inland Mission* [CIM, 1900]).

5. Ibid., p. 15.

6. Paul A. Cohen, 'The Contested Past: the Boxers as History and Myth', *Journal of Asian Studies* (February 1992), pp. 82–113.

7. Hefley, *By Their Blood*.

8. Quoted in Hefley, *By Their Blood*, pp. 37–38.

9. In *Journal of Asian Studies*, vol. 20 (February 1962), pp. 169ff.

10. Ibid., pp. 176–177. This inflammatory accusation was apparently common.

11. Ibid., p. 169.

12. James and Marti Hefley in an article at www.crossroad.to/Persecution/Martyrs/Boxer

13. Hefley, *By Their Blood*, p. 26.

14. See Broomhall, *The Martyred Missionaries of the China Inland Mission*.

15. In Dr J. Hudon Taylor, *Hudson Taylor's Spiritual Secret* (Moody Press, 1932), p.135.

16. Brother Yun, *The Heavenly Man*, p. 22.

17. Ibid., pp. 110–115. Used by permission.

18. Ibid.

19. Rick Warren, *Purpose Driven Life* (Zondervan, 2002), p. 51.

20. David Aikman, *Jesus in Beijing* (Monarch Publications, 2005). First published in USA by Regnery Publishing, 2003.

## Chapter 12: Church of Martyrs – Islamic Persecution

1. Foucauld, *Discipline and Punish*, p. 47.

2. Bertrand Russell, *Theory and Practice of Bolshevism* (London, 1921), p. 29.

3. *The Times*, 7th February 2005.

4. Bahdawi (*c.* 1290), in Ibn Warraq, *Why I am not a Muslim*.

5. See Christopher Hitchen's cover notes, ibid.

6. Ibid., p. 174.

7. Ibid.

8. Voice of the Martyrs is a charity working for human rights (see www.vom.org). This story and several like it can be found in *Jesus Freaks II*.

9. Ibid., pp. 30ff.

10. Quoted in Hefley, *By Their Blood*, p. 226.

11. Anthony Browne, 'Church of Martyrs', cover story in the *Spectator*, April 2005.

## Chapter 13: For Such a Time as This

1. Preface to Dr J. Hudson Taylor, *Hudson Taylor's Spiritual Secret*, p. 9.

2. *Independent on Sunday*, 4th April 2004.

3. *Guardian*, 10th April 2004.

4. *Le Monde*, editorial 31st March 2004: '*Alors que partout gagne l'extrémisme religieux, ce film peut avoir des effets dévastateurs. . .Comment s'étonner que les soutines de Gibson se trouvent dans les rangs de catholiques traditionalistes pour qui la culpabilité des juifs dans la mort de Jésus ne fait aucun doute. Ce film rejoint les pires tendances fondamentalistes du mone moderne.*'

5. Mel Gibson: Introduction to *The Passion of the Christ*.

6. Naissance et Tourments du Protestantisme français 1997, Ed. Michel Gosse.

7. Ed. André Fabre, 'Marie Durand', *La Cause*, 1972.

8. See *Le Theatre Sacré des Cévennes* (Edtns de Paris 1978) and Jean Cavalier, *Mémoires sur la guerre des Camisards* (Edtns Payot 1973).

9. Migault's journal: *Narrative of the Sufferings of a Protestant Family* (London 1824), p. 37.

10. Frontispiece to *Hudson Taylor's Spiritual Secret*.